Pietro's Book

THE STORY OF
A TUSCAN PEASANT

Pietro's Book

THE STORY OF
A TUSCAN PEASANT

Pietro Pinti & Jenny Bawtree

CONSTABLE • LONDON

Dedico questo libro ai miei genitori Sabatino e Concetta,
e a tutti i contadini che come loro riuscirono ad allevare
i loro figli con dignità, nonostante la loro povertà.

I dedicate this book to my parents, Sabatino and Concetta,
and to all peasants who, like them, managed to bring up their
children with dignity, notwithstanding their poverty.

Pietro

Constable & Robinson Ltd
3 The Lanchesters
162 Fulham Palace Road
London, W6 9ER
www.constablerobinson.com

First published in Great Britain by Constable,
an imprint of Constable & Robinson Ltd, 2003

Copyright © Pietro Pinti and Jenny Bawtree 2003

The right of Pietro Pinti and Jenny Bawtree to be identified as the authors of
this work has been asserted by them in accordance with the
Copyright, Designs and Patents Act 1988

A copy of the British Library Cataloguing in Publication Data is
available from the British Library

ISBN 1-84119-730-0

Printed and bound in the EU

Contents

List of Illustrations   vii
Introduction   1

1   The Pinti Family   15
2   At Work   39
3   Fascism and the War   65
4   After the Armistice   83
5   A Year in the Life of a *Contadino*   103
6   Pastimes and Feast Days   139
7   After the War   161

    Glossary   179

Illustrations

Map of the Arno valley (drawing by James Harris)   4

Two maps drawn in 1584 (State Archives, Florence, Italy)   8

Sixteenth-century map of Nusenna (State Archives, Florence, Italy)   18

Il Casino del Monte, the house where Pietro was born (drawing by James Harris)   26

Military map showing Mercatale and its surroundings   30

Class photograph dating from Pietro's time   34

La Casa del Bosco, the house where Pietro spent most of his working life (drawing by James Harris)   42

Sabatino, Pietro's father   44

Girl spinning with distaff (© Copyright 1982 by CASA EDITRICE BONECHI s.r.l.)   52

Concetta, Pietro's mother   56

Azeglio, Pietro's brother, serving as a groom in the Italian army   72

Ploughing with oxen   78

A yoke for a pair of oxen (© Copyright 1982 by CASA EDITRICE BONECHI s.r.l.)   106

Pietro prunes the olives   111

Threshing   119

Pietro with his oxen   123

Olive-picking (drawing by James Harris)   133

Pietro at the age of 29   173

Pietro and Franca on their wedding day   176

Introduction

Ever since the nineteenth century the Tuscan countryside has cast a spell on the Anglo-Saxon mind. The poets of the Romantic movement began to contemplate not only their own landscape with new eyes, but also that of other European countries. On their journeys towards Italy, long since the Mecca of artists and writers, they were first struck by the savage majesty of the Alps, and then lowered their eyes, perhaps with relief, to the softer, more domesticated beauty of the Tuscan countryside. In many ways it differed from the English landscape they knew: the gently undulating hills of England, with their extensive cornfields, patches of woodland and green pastures sprinkled with cattle and sheep, hardly resemble the more rugged Tuscan countryside, with its vineyards, olive groves and vast areas of forest. Yet the two landscapes have one thing in common: they are the fruit of a collaboration between man and nature over three thousand years or more. Consequently, they are landscapes that do not inspire awe, rather they reassure us. Poets such as Byron, Shelley, Elizabeth Barrett Browning were all captivated by the gentle beauty of the Tuscan countryside and celebrated it in many of their poems. In the following century it inspired works by D.H. Lawrence, Aldous Huxley, E.M. Forster, Virginia Woolf and many more.

None of these writers, however, settled for any length of time in the Tuscan countryside. They saw it from the gardens of Florentine villas or on their travels by carriage or car from one city to another.

As a result, their appreciation was mostly of what they saw, not what lay behind it. It was not until the 1960s that a new generation of writers began to celebrate the Tuscan landscape from quite a different viewpoint. It was during this period that Tuscan peasant farmers began to leave the land, attracted by jobs available in the towns during the economic boom. Their picturesque farmhouses, many of them dating back several centuries, fell empty and the landowners, unaware of their value, sold them off to foreigners for absurdly small sums. Among these were a handful of English writers and artists. Because the houses needed restoring, these expatriates found themselves dealing daily with the local builders, carpenters and plumbers. Moreover, as a few hectares of vineyard and olive grove usually came with the house, they also had to seek advice from the local farmers about how to tend them. These experiences led to books that not only celebrated the beauty of the countryside in which the writers had opted to settle, but also talked about the local people and the farming traditions of the area.

Rural Tuscany is brought even closer to us, however, in *Pietro's Book* because it is written not by a foreign intellectual but by a Tuscan peasant. In its way, this book, too, is a celebration of the Tuscan countryside, dwelling not so much on the beauty of the landscape as on how that beauty was created. When we read Pietro's description of the wine harvest, we see in our mind's eye the vines that hung in graceful curves from tree to tree, the white oxen harnessed to carts, waiting patiently at the end of the vineyard. He tells us how he pruned the olives, and we can imagine the peasants poking their ladders up among the silver branches of those age-old trees while the womenfolk gathered the prunings into bundles. He describes how as a child he used to accompany the pigs into the woods in search of acorns, and we can visualize those forests of oak and chestnut, with their dense undergrowth of arbutus, broom and juniper, stretching up over the rolling hills towards the horizon.

We learn, too, about the way of life of those who have created this landscape: the generations of peasants who, like Pietro, have dedicated not only their labour but also their love to this blessed land. The people Pietro describes are simple and often illiterate, but with their manual skills, sense of humour and fondness for music and storytelling, they have a culture of their own which only now, as it slowly dies, people are beginning to appreciate.

Pietro and I wrote this book together. It was a coincidence that we met. Born and educated in England, I came to Italy in 1964 to teach English in Florence. The following year my sister, who was working in Rome, bought our parents a house above the village of Mercatale in the Arno valley, thirty miles from Florence. Pietro was our neighbour and soon became a family friend.

The Arno valley, locally called the Valdarno, is unfamiliar to the average tourist, who prefers to visit the nearby cities of Florence, Siena and Arezzo. Nevertheless, as I discovered over the years, there are countless sites of historical interest in the valley, largely due to its geographical position. Protected to the east by Pratomagno, a long mountain ridge, and to the west by the Chianti hills, the Valdarno is a broad, fertile valley, pleasantly wooded. The river Arno is not large but many streams flow into it, so when there is heavy rain it is subject to flooding. It was for this reason that the ancient highways, first traced by the Etruscans and then by the Romans, ran along the base of the mountains on either side of the valley rather than along the valley floor. In consequence most of the ancient settlements were to be found along those roads.

Villages on both sides of the valley continued to grow during the Middle Ages and local warlords erected castles to defend them. From the twelfth century onwards this rich agricultural land was contested by the cities of Florence, Arezzo and Siena and it was only then that towns like Montevarchi and San Giovanni grew up in the bottom of the valley: originally market-places, they were developed and fortified by the Florentine Republic in its struggle for dominance over its rivals.

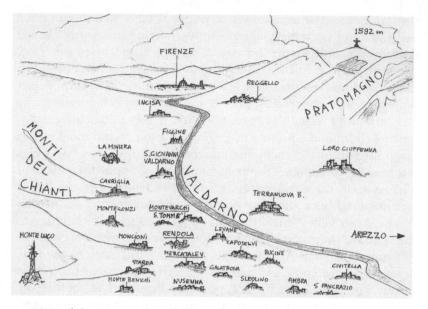

Map of the Arno valley, showing the places mentioned in the book.

The Etruscans settled principally in the southern part of Tuscany and in Latium, north of Rome. There are, however, traces of their presence in the vicinity of Mercatale Valdarno, the village that Pietro refers to most frequently in this book. The hill that rises behind the village is dominated by the ruins of a medieval castle, but its name, Galatrona, reveals its Etruscan origin, and it is probable that an Etruscan settlement existed up there. For safety's sake the Etruscans used to live on the tops of hills.

The Romans too left traces in the area. Close to the old part of Mercatale there is an area which retains the name *il campo romano*, the Roman field. When new houses were built there in the 1970s, the remains of Roman walls and other artefacts were found. The presence of a Roman settlement is explained by the fact that on the slopes of Galatrona hill ran an important Roman road, the Cassia Adrianea: it was built by the Emperor Hadrian in AD 123 as an alternative to part of the more ancient Cassia Vetus on the other side of the Arno valley. Next to the road where it passes under the hill of Galatrona there was a *praetorium*, the residence of the Roman military governor. The name of the eighteenth-century villa built on the spot, 'Petrolo', derives from the Latin word. The remains of Roman walls indicate that there was also a Roman settlement on top of the hill where the medieval tower now stands. The Roman road descended to Mercatale and then passed through the area where the medieval village of Rendola now stands, before proceeding in the direction of Florence.

The farmhouse which my sister bought was called Le Muricce di Sopra, but in order not to confuse it with a nearby farm called Le Muricce, we immediately baptized it La Casa del Bosco – the house of the woods. Along with the house my sister purchased about ten acres of field and woodland, and now owned about three hundred olive trees and a few dozen vines. We had no idea, of course, how to look after them, as our father's experience of farming in England was limited to pigs and cereals. It was therefore providential that we met our neighbour Pietro quite early on. He had come to plough the land next to ours with a pair of big white oxen. We were struck at once by his kindly smile and the affability with which he welcomed us, a family of foreigners who spoke his language with a strong English accent. He explained that he now lived close to Mercatale, but that he had spent thirty years at Casa del Bosco and had been born up at Casino del Monte, only five hundred yards away. In fact, his oxen had been reared at Casa del Bosco, and when he ploughed the field near the house he had to be careful not to let them veer into our dining room: previously it had been their stable. I remember asking Pietro what his oxen were called, and he replied, ' "Left" and "Right", so that when I harness them to the plough I know which side to put them'.

Soon we became friends and Pietro often came to see us. We began to ask his advice about a number of things: whom we should call to prune the olives (he made it clear right from the start that it was no work for novices), how we should look after the vines and what we could plant in the heavy, stony soil, so unlike that of our own country. Then as now he was always ready to interrupt his work in order to give us some advice, or simply to have a chat. After all, like all peasants he worked from dawn to dusk and considered it normal to allow himself a pause from time to time.

In the course of our conversations Pietro told us that he was a *mezzadro*, and he explained to us what *mezzadria* involved: it was an agricultural system which was for us a complete novelty. A landowner would assign to the *mezzadro* a *podere*, which consisted of a farmhouse and on average ten to fifteen hectares of land surrounding it (the size of the smallholding varied from place to place). The landowner would provide the implements, the seed and so on, while the *mezzadro* would supply the labour. Then the produce of the farm, the oil, the wine, the grain and all the rest, would be shared out equally between the landowner and the *mezzadro* ('*mezzo*' actually means 'half'). It seems fair in theory, but in practice it meant that the farmer had to work from dawn to dusk just in order to keep his family fed and clothed: he had no possibility of saving money for a rainy day. A landowner, on the other hand, usually possessed several farms and was able to sell most of his share of the produce, growing rich in the process. He was therefore less affected by a bad harvest, while the *mezzadro* was hard hit: a ten-minute hailstorm could ruin his grapes, a late frost could destroy the olive flowers and jeopardize that year's olive crop. While some landowners were enlightened and did their best to alleviate the harsh conditions under which the farmers lived, most seemed deliberately to ignore them. The system dated back to the Middle Ages and it is incredible to think that the last *mezzadria* contracts expired only a few years ago.

During the Middle Ages the peasants in this area were small landowners. They lived in houses huddled together for safety in villages and walked daily to their scattered parcels of land, a vineyard here, an olive grove there. They were desperately poor by any standards: only the 'wealthy' ones owned an ox or an ass. It was in the sixteenth century, a period of relative peace and prosperity, that the old feudal families of Tuscany realized that they could obtain high profits from the sale of agricultural produce, in particular grain, wine and olive oil. They began to buy up the land of the small peasant farmers and to build the first *case coloniche*, destined to house the *mezzadri*. The same phenomenon occurred in the area of Montevarchi, where the middle classes had acquired wealth by means of commercial enterprises. And so the *podere*, the farmhouse surrounded by a few hectares of land, came into being, and with it the *mezzadria* system. Most of these houses retain their medieval aspect; others, the *case leopoldine*, houses designed by architects in the eighteenth century during the rule of Leopold I, Grand Duke of Tuscany, are much more spacious, adopting, however, the traditional characteristics of the earlier houses with their arches, balconies, outside staircases and pigeon lofts. In some ways the peasant was better off than before, as now he had the use of a larger house and land conveniently located around it. But, on the other hand, he found himself at the mercy of a landlord who in most cases exploited his industriousness. And this state of affairs lasted until the 1980s, though by then many *mezzadri* had already left the land.

In the sixteenth century the Grand Duchy of Florence drew up maps to control and maintain the public highways. These showed the new farmhouses and also the churches which appear in Pietro's narrative, those at Mercatale, Caposelvi, Galatrona, La Torre and Rendola, all built during the Middle Ages. The most important was the church of Galatrona which, being a *pieve*, was the only one with a baptismal font, and it was there that the bishop stayed when he made his pastoral visits. Beside each church there was a *canonica* where the priest resided, and attached to it or nearby were one or more *poderi* whose farmers gave half their produce to the priest. The church of Galatrona possessed seven *poderi* and was therefore the richest parish of all. One of these *poderi* was in the mountain village of Nusenna where Pietro's parents were born. His father, however, ran the farm which belonged to the village priest.

With the development of the *mezzadria* system came the con-struction of *case padronali*, the landowners' country houses. Fam-ilies of noble birth, already in possession of large estates even though they now lived mostly in town, converted their castles into comfortable mansions, or in some cases built mansions from scratch. So the *fattorie* were born, still a feature of today's agricultural system, especially in the Chianti. The word derives from *fattore*, roughly equivalent to our farm bailiff; in fact, the landowner would often spend only the summer months at his *casa padronale*. For the rest of the year he would entrust the adminis-tration of his estate to his *fattore*, coming to the country only occasionally to examine the accounts. The *fattoria* developed later in the Arno valley, perhaps because it was some distance from the

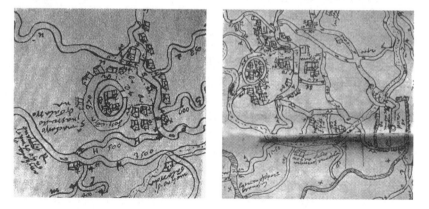

Two maps drawn in 1584: on the left the castle and village of Galatrona, on the right a castle and its market: La Torre on the left and the square of Mercatale on the right.

major cities of the area, Florence, Arezzo and Siena. The largest *fattoria* in the Mercatale area was that of Rendola: the *casa padronale* was built by the Firidolfi-Ricasolis, the most powerful family in the Chianti. No doubt the baron of the time was aware that in this area the land was more fertile than his own and was also closer to the markets. At the end of the eighteenth century the property passed into the hands of Conte Carnavaro, a relation of the Ricasolis. When Pietro was a *mezzadro*, the *fattoria* of Rendola was one of the largest in the Arno valley, with its great cellars, its storehouses, its thirty-four *poderi* and its vast woodlands. It was only in the fifties that it began to go downhill, largely as a result of mismanagement, hastened by the winds of social change. To pay the debts that had accrued many of the *poderi* were sold, often to the peasants who worked them. Finally the *fattoria* itself was sold to two families, who divided the villa into two separate dwellings and shared out the few *poderi* that remained.

The tough conditions under which a *mezzadro* lived were brought home to me when I went to visit Pietro in his own home. We had supper in the kitchen, which in those days served as a living room as well. It consisted of a long table, benches, a *madia*, a piece of furniture in which the bread was kneaded, a *cucina economica*, a kind of wood stove, a few shelves: the bare essentials. Over the fire on the hearth was a large copper cauldron hanging from a chain, so that there was always hot water available. In the bedrooms there was no form of heating whatsoever: once I helped Pietro's wife Franca carry Sergio, their younger son, to bed and the cold in the bedroom made me catch my breath. There was no proper lavatory, only a tiny room containing a wooden seat with a hole in it: this led to the *pozzo nero*, the black hole, into which flowed the liquid manure from the stables. And I wondered to myself: how could the owner of the house not be ashamed to provide a house in this condition, in the sixties when bathrooms and central heating were taken for granted in urban areas? I learnt later that most *mezzadri* lived in this way.

When I was researching this book I came across a fifteenth-century inventory which lists the possessions of a certain Domenico di Agnolo of Galatrona, a huddle of buildings on the hill above Mercatale. The furniture of his kitchen consisted of a table, a bench and a *madia*, while in the fireplace there was a copper cauldron hanging from a chain. Almost exactly the contents of Pietro's kitchen five hundred years later: only the wood stove was a modern addition.

It is not surprising, then, that shortly after we first met Pietro and his family they did what so many other *mezzadri* were doing: left their farm and moved to the nearest town. Italy was recovering from the war and there was an economic boom. Small factories were springing up all over the place and there was work for all. Blocks of flats were built on the outskirts of towns. The flats were cheap and it was possible to buy them by paying monthly instalments. So Pietro bought a flat at Pestello, on the outskirts of Montevarchi, and, like many other peasants, took a job as a builder's mate: they were, after all, no strangers to backbreaking toil. At the age of forty-two he began to receive a weekly pay-packet for the first time. Working hours were long and it took him over an hour to reach his workplace. Nevertheless, every weekend Pietro drove up to Casa del Bosco to help us with our small farm. Evidently he was still drawn to the land, and for a few years he lovingly tended our vines and olive trees which he had for so many years tended for his *padrone*.

In 1966 I bought a small grey mare, Sheba, and at weekends I rode round the surrounding woods and fields. The locals were amazed to see a woman on horseback, an unheard-of sight in those days: some were even scandalized ('She rides with her legs apart, has she no sense of shame?'). I discovered how beautiful the countryside was and how plentiful were the trails, ideal for trekking. So I decided to give up teaching and set up a riding centre. Having rented an abandoned farmhouse near the village of Rendola, only fifteen minutes' walk from Casa del Bosco, I bought a few what I now realize were rather nondescript horses and I pronounced the riding centre open. Fortunately the novelty appealed to the local people and the venture proved an instant success. Clients both young and less young flocked to Rendola from all over the Arno valley. Soon the work became too much for one person, so I asked Pietro if he would come and help me at weekends. The clientele continued to grow, so much so that a year later I offered Pietro a permanent job and he accepted.

Now it is more than thirty years that he and I have been working side by side. With the help of Pietro and later his son Sergio, I managed to create a flourishing business, offering hospitality in my house in addition to the riding. When the need arose Pietro turned out to be a born cook, not only recreating the dishes his mother prepared in his childhood, but inventing new ones as well. His cooking and the stories he tells over the dinner table are quite as much of an attraction as the horses. When Pietro is not in the kitchen he is to be found in the vegetable garden, digging, weeding and planting, always a farmer at heart.

From the beginning of our friendship I loved hearing about Pietro's life, and he enjoyed recounting it just as much. He claims, with reason, 'My generation has had a unique experience: we were born in the Middle Ages and now we are living in the age of computers.' In fact, no generation has seen such dramatic changes in so short a time. When Pietro was a child in the 1930s, his family lived in conditions of extreme poverty. His mother did the cooking over the fire in the hearth, and that fire was also the sole form of heating for the house. Everything the family ate was produced on the farm and olive-oil lamps were used to see by after dusk. The women would spin wool and hemp from the farm and made clothes for the entire family. It was a way of life that had not changed, except in a few minor aspects, for the last five hundred years.

Over the years Pietro told me all about his life as a *mezzadro* – without bitterness, even with a certain nostalgia. He had certainly worked hard, but his labour had brought with it a great deal of satisfaction. At that time there were no other prospects anyway, he had no choice but resign himself to his lot. Moments of leisure were few and therefore all the more to be savoured. Pietro nevertheless found time to play the trumpet and the mouth organ, write songs and poems, read: his favourite book is *The Divine Comedy*, which he keeps on his bedside table as others keep the Bible. And notwithstanding his poverty he has always maintained a great sense of humour, as is characteristic of most Tuscans. All the years I have known him Pietro has told stories about knights and brigands or about people he has met in his daily life: the blacksmith, the carter, the shopkeeper, the priest, the basket-maker. Poor folk most of them, and yet the stories are merry ones, such as true Tuscans are wont to tell: they are capable of issuing wisecracks even on their deathbeds. Even when he talks about the Second World War, a period that brought atrocious suffering to the Tuscan people, Pietro manages to recount amusing episodes.

The more I listened to Pietro the more I began to realize that all this information was of inestimable value, because it belonged to a peasant culture which is rapidly dying. Once Pietro's generation has passed away we shall no longer have any contacts with the way of life he describes. It risks being lost for ever. Of course there are archives, and other peasants have told their stories before Pietro: but not with his acute powers of observation and his pervading sense of humour. So I bought a tape recorder and together we began to record his life story. He obviously relished the prospect of a wider audience and told his story with renewed gusto. We worked on the tapes during the winter evenings when we had little else to do. Every time we completed a tape my son and I copied it out laboriously on our old typewriter and then put the pages into a folder entitled 'Pietro's Book'. Years passed, some winters we wrote a lot, others hardly anything: like all people who rise early in the morning we often felt drowsy in the evening and did not feel like getting down to work. Then I bought a computer and the process speeded up. Finally I plucked up courage and began to arrange the material into a book, following more or less a chronological order. I had no trouble in choosing a title: we had already been referring to 'Pietro's' for years.

This is, of course, the story of a peasant, not a professor. Historical events are presented from Pietro's viewpoint, and no doubt there are some inaccuracies, some unconventional interpretations, some biased judgements. But Pietro recounts his version of history and I have tried to be faithful to it and to our main aim, to create a lasting memorial to a way of life that has all but disappeared.

What will happen when Pietro's generation passes on? During the 1960s there was a general exodus from the land and Tuscan agriculture is still suffering the consequences. If the government had given more importance to agriculture instead of concentrating on industry, if landowners had had the foresight to occupy themselves more with the wellbeing of the peasants, we wouldn't be witnessing the state of abandon which characterizes some of the agricultural land of Tuscany today. It is true that by adopting modern business methods most big estates have managed to survive, even to prosper. They have planted big 'industrial' vineyards, they have learnt to market their produce, and they have wisely taken advantage of the financial aid provided by the Common Market. As for the farmhouses that have been abandoned by the peasants, they have restored them for *agriturismo*, that is to say they rent them out to tourists (often at astronomical prices). Other houses have been bought by foreigners and transformed into luxurious homes, usually, though not always, with exquisite taste. Before the influx of foreigners which resulted in the hiking of prices, a certain number of peasants were able to buy their *poderi*. But they are now growing old, and find it more and more difficult to look after their land. You rarely see anyone less than sixty years old in the countryside: only perhaps at weekends, when their sons, who have already found more lucrative work elsewhere, give them a hand with the pruning and picking.

When I ride round the more remote areas of the countryside I often see abandoned fields and houses that have fallen into ruin. Where man has retreated the woods invade: the vines are swallowed by the undergrowth and swathes of brambles hang from the olive trees. No one would wish to return to the old *mezzadria* system, to the poverty and toil that were the peasants' daily lot. Yet the sight of this land that is no longer loved and tended fills me with melancholy.

Jenny Bawtree
Rendola 2003

CHAPTER 1

The Pinti Family

My parents were born in Nusenna. They say the Etruscans once settled there. This small village is situated on the eastern slopes of the Chianti hills and looks down on to the Arno valley. To reach it you go to Mercatale Valdarno and then take a little road that follows the stream called Tricesimo. After a couple of miles the road ascends among dense woods of oak and chestnut. Following a number of steep bends you reach Nusenna. The village lies halfway between Mercatale and Monteluco, the highest point of this area of the Chianti hills, where the ruins of a castle of the same name lie hidden in the undergrowth. On top of the mountain there is now a tall television transmitter, visible for miles around; but it used to be a wild place covered with impenetrable forest, where only fifty years earlier you ran the risk of running into bandits.

Now the road to Nusenna is asphalted, but it was only a dirt track when I was a boy. At the beginning of the 1930s the village was much the same as it had been for several centuries: a group of nondescript houses huddled round a square, where a church of no particular architectural interest barely stands out from the other buildings. The village was surrounded by fields and farmland, and wooded hills stretched as far as the horizon.

My family left Nusenna in 1908 and went to live on a farm near Mercatale. But many of our relations still lived in Nusenna and I often went to visit them, so I remember the village well.

The square at Nusenna was roughly circular, and to enter the village there were two gates which were so narrow that a cart could barely scrape through. During the Second World War the gates were blown up by the Germans, in order to block the road. They did the same thing in other villages, too. But the gates were still standing when I was a small boy. Most of the houses were within the village walls, but a few were scattered here and there in the surrounding countryside.

Almost everyone at Nusenna owned their own small piece of land. No big landowners lived there, perhaps because it was in such an isolated position they would not have wanted to. There were only two families of *mezzadri*, those living in a farmhouse that belonged to the priest of Galatrona, and my parents, who worked for the priest of Nusenna. At that time all the priests had *mezzadri* to work for them, otherwise how would they have got enough to eat? They didn't work themselves! I must add, however, that they didn't have a stipend as they do now, and that some of them were very poor.

The other farmers all had their own land – they grew corn and cultivated vines and olive trees. They also had a number of sheep, as the grass grew well all the year round. It wasn't too hot in the summer like down in the valley. But most of the time they worked in the woods. They used to make charcoal, which they then sold to the carters, Giusto, Mario and Pancana. Giusto was my cousin, because his mother was my father's sister. The carters used to take the charcoal down to Montevarchi and sell it to the families there. Charcoal was more practical than wood because it took up less space: ten quintals of wood made a quintal of charcoal. And charcoal makes less smoke when you burn it. The inhabitants of Nusenna used to make bundles of tree heather and they sold these also to the carters, who took them down to the brick kiln at Montevarchi. There bricks and various kinds of roof tile were made. Tree heather burns very quickly, so goodness knows how many bundles went into the oven every day.

Then there were the *marroni* chestnuts which were sold for boiling or toasting over the fire. Every farmer had his own parcel of woodland and picked the *marroni* in October or November, according to the weather. The carter bought these too and took them down to Montevarchi. Poor things, they had nothing down in the town and had to buy everything, not like us farmers who didn't have to buy anything at all.

The carters loaded as much as possible on to their carts in order to make fewer journeys, so the horses had a hard time of it, but at least the road between Nusenna and Mercatale went downhill all the way. The only problem was the steep hill you had to come up when you left Mercatale. If the cart was heavily loaded the horse couldn't pull it up, in which case the carters would travel in pairs. When they reached the steep hill they unharnessed one of the horses and attached it to the other cart so that the horses could pull side by side. When they reached the top they would unharness both horses, lead them back down and harness them both to the other cart. It all took a lot of time, but people weren't in a hurry in those days.

On the return journey the carters had money in their pockets and they would stop at the *botteghe* to have a drink. There was one at Pestello, just outside Montevarchi, and another at Mercatale. They usually got a bit tipsy so it was a good thing that their horses knew the way home. They were a rough lot – it's not surprising that we say to someone who is behaving badly, 'You're worse than a carter.'

The story goes that Muschio, a carter from La Torre, was returning from Montevarchi but didn't stop at the *bottega* at Pestello. Pancana of Nusenna was driving the cart behind him and asked, 'Aren't we drinking this evening?' 'I haven't even a *centesimo!*' 'I'll pay!' said Pancana, so Muschio shouted to his horse: 'Well, then, whoooooaaa!' and pulled the reins. After that, 'Well, then, whoooaaa' became a local saying.

The life people led at Nusenna seems hard to us now. But they

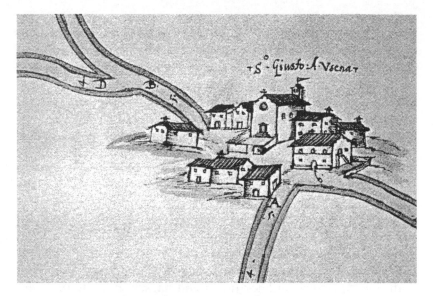

Sixteenth-century map of Nusenna.

thought themselves well off, with all those woods round them. And except for the *mezzadri* of the priest, they had no master to tell them what to do and that was a fine thing indeed.

I don't know when the Pintis came to Nusenna. I believe they came originally from the Chianti, because we still have relations there. In my grandfather's time they were in the Maremma in the south of Tuscany, I know this because my father used to tell us how my grandfather took food to Stoppa, the famous Maremman bandit. It's possible that the Pintis were Florentines once, because there is a street called Borgo Pinti behind the cathedral. Who knows, perhaps the Pintis were nobles once if a street was named after them? Then they lost all their money and had to go into the country and become peasants. But that's just an idea of mine, maybe they've always been peasants after all.

My family came down from Nusenna in 1908. There was my

father, my mother and my father's brothers, Domenico and Pietro, both with their wives, and then there were all the children. I don't remember much about my uncles, they died when I was small. I know that Pietro and my father fought in the First World War. They were in the Engineers, making trenches. Farmers, after all, were used to digging. My father returned safe and sound, but Pietro got tuberculosis and died at home not long afterwards. His name is on a monument to the fallen down at Montevarchi. It gives me a strange feeling to see my name written there in the marble. Domenico had a stroke and then he died too.

My family came down from Nusenna because the farm was too small, while Casino del Monte, their new farm, had ten hectares or more, with land stretching down to the main road along the River Tricesimo. Mostly vines and olives grew there, but there was also plenty of land for sowing grain, and an area of woodland too. More than enough to support three families!

We often returned to Nusenna to visit my grandmother. We went along the same road as we do now. However, I remember taking a lot of short cuts from bend to bend, too steep for the carts but easy on foot. It was an hour and a half's journey, but we were used to walking. My uncle and aunt lived with my grandmother, together with their three children, Vasco, Vaio and Fedora. We all ate lunch together and then we went to fetch the water. There was no water in Nusenna. Everyone went to get their water from a spring called Leccio near Reggioli, a farm nearly half a mile from the village. We filled up our flasks and copper pitchers and then lugged them back to Nusenna, wondering why they had not built the village closer to the only source of water.

My grandmother lived at the bottom end of the square. You had to climb some stairs to her house. The baker had his oven on the ground floor, which must have helped to keep her rooms warm when it was lit. She had a *bottega* at the top end of the square where she sold a bit of everything: tobacco, sugar, sweets and pasta. In those days pasta was sold loose, not in packets like now. People would also buy cigarettes one or two at a time. They could not have afforded a whole packet. The shop was also a kind of bar and meeting place with a few tables, where the villagers could go to have a glass of wine and play cards. They did not drink coffee, it was not the custom then. Sometimes my grandmother sold a kind of coffee made of barley: it was called *estratto di vecchina*, old lady's extract, on the packet there was a picture of an old lady holding a distaff. You put a lump of this into boiling water and the water turned black, making it look like real coffee. It was supposed to be good for you, which was probably why they had an old lady on the packet. Even she could drink it! It was popular at that time – we didn't have coffee made from coffee beans till after the war.

I didn't know my cousins very well. They were much older than I was. Fedora married and went to live in Siena, Vasco played the mandolin and became a customs officer in Florence. Only Varo remained in Nusenna to run the shop. I also had a second cousin called Bibo. I remember a story about him. When I was eight I went to be confirmed at Nusenna so that my grandmother could be present at the ceremony. In those days when you were confirmed they put a ribbon round your head, tied in a knot at the back. It was white and had a cross on the front made of sequins. You had to wear it for three or four days. In some places you had to wear it for a month, in which case you had one ribbon for weekdays and one for Sundays, so that you would always go to church with a clean ribbon. The story went round that you wore a ribbon because the bishop put a nail into your forehead. I thought this couldn't be true, but I had my doubts. I thought to myself: what kind of nail is he going to use? If it was one of those tintacks people use when they are making baskets, that wouldn't be too bad. But if it was the one you put into the seeder to block the wings, that was a foot long, it would come out of the other side of your head! But basically I knew that the story couldn't be true. My second cousin Bibo believed it, though. He was a stocky chap who was always hungry and that winter he had eaten all the dried figs that his mother had prepared for Christmas. So his family said to him, 'You wait, young rascal, the bishop'll fix you when he puts that nail through your head!'

On Confirmation Day Bibo didn't want to go into the church. His father and his uncle had to run after him all round the square. In the end they trapped him behind my cousin's cart and dragged him towards the church. But he still put up a struggle, bracing his hands and feet against the doorway. They almost snapped off his arms trying to get him in! But things turned out well for Bibo. The bishop didn't put a nail through his head, he just tied a white ribbon round it as he did with the rest of us.

The priests tried to explain religion to us, but we were a bit slow and we didn't always understand what they were getting at. I remember a boy who went to the priest to be tested before his confirmation, and the priest asked him, 'How many commandments are there?' The boy didn't know the answer, but he thought, well, God says we can't do all sorts of things, so he answered, 'A hundred!' And the priest gave him a cuff. As the boy ran out of the church he met a friend of his who was coming in. He asked him: 'How many commandments are there, actually?' 'There are ten,' replied his friend. 'Don't you tell him there are ten,' said the first boy. 'I said a hundred and he gave me a cuff. If you say ten he'll give you a thrashing!'

I didn't understand much about religion either. When I took Communion for the first time I believed the holy wafer was soaked in *vinsanto*, a kind of sweet wine, and I longed for my turn. But when the priest put the wafer on my tongue it stuck to my palate. I couldn't get it unstuck, and it didn't taste of *vinsanto* at all! What a disappointment. And then I saw it was the priest who drank the *vinsanto*, lucky devil. I hadn't understood at all what Communion meant – all the prayers were in Latin and I was too shy to ask the priest to explain the words.

When my parents came down from Nusenna they already had two children, Bruna and Azeglio. Then my mother gave birth another ten times, but four of the babies died. Whether they were stillborn or died later I was never told. We didn't talk about such things. The babies were buried in the cemetery but there was no funeral because they hadn't been baptized. Having children was a woman's lot and she had to rear them all. It was considered to be God's will. If one of them died, people would say, 'Thank goodness, otherwise how could she have managed, poor woman?' If a family couldn't afford to keep all their children they would send one of the boys to be a *garzone* in another family. They would not be paid for their work, but at least they would be fed and clothed. Daughters were sent to more wealthy families to be maidservants, even at twelve years of age.

After Bruna and Azeglio came Marsiglia, Nunzia, Vittoria, Silvia and Azeglia. They were all born at home, as was the custom, and the midwife supervised the birth. The doctor only came if it was a difficult delivery, but then the mother usually died anyway. Next came Natalia, whom my parents took from the Ospedale degli Innocenti, an orphanage in Florence. The orphans were certainly innocent, poor little things, their parents less so. The children were almost all abandoned because they were illegitimate. Many peasants adopted these *innocentini* because the hospital gave them a subsidy and this helped to feed the other children as well.

As soon as the children were born their father had to register them at the town hall. A man from Mercatale once gave the same name, Assunta, to two of his daughters. He had so many children, I suppose he couldn't remember all their names. Then there was another fellow who had a vineyard near the wood at Gretole, under the *fattoria* of Sinciano, and he lived in a hut with his wife and children. Later on he moved to a proper house on the road to Montevarchi. When there was the census, officials from the town hall went round all the houses to get information about the families living there. But when they went to this family they found a son who hadn't been registered at all. The boy certainly didn't know when he was born, and they all sat there scratching their heads when the father suddenly had an inspiration. 'I remember the day now,' he said. 'People were coming down from Sinciano on their way to Montevarchi market, so it must have been a Thursday!'

I was the last child to be born. It was in 1927, when my mother was forty-four years old. She probably didn't expect to give birth again after so many children. She must have been glad to have had another son after all those daughters. Years later I wrote an *ottava rima* about the event:

Nacqui di primavera un giorno ricordato	I was born on a special day in spring
In una casa vicino alla foresta,	In a house close to the forest,
Era il primo aprile, l'ho già accennato,	It was April 1st, as I told you,
E stava per fiorire la ginestra.	And the broom was about to flower.
Mio padre era un mezzadro diseredato	My father was a poor sharecropper
Però si dice fece una gran festa,	But they say he celebrated that day,
Perché il giorno delle chiapperelle	Because on April Fool's Day
E' nato un maschio dopo sei sorelle.	A son was born after six sisters.

Males were stronger than females and they could do the heavy work on the farm, though of course the women had to play their part too. Goodness me, they all worked like slaves, not like young people nowadays who study till they are twenty years old and even after that they often don't go to work. In my day if my mother saw you doing nothing she would send you to cut the wood or draw water from the fountain.

One member of our family died when he was only twenty years old. That was my cousin Dionigi, Domenico's son. He used to drive the oxen, and one day he had to take a load of firewood to the *padrone*. Oxen move very slowly and there was a *tramontana*, a strong cold wind blowing from the north. He had a touch of flu already so he got pneumonia. Poor people didn't usually call the doctor because you had to pay him and there was little money to spare, but this time they called him because the boy was very ill, even though they had put a mustard poultice on his chest. The doctor lived in Bucine, which was three miles away, and he came on his bicycle. But he couldn't do much because there were no antibiotics then, and the boy died. I was four years old at the time, but I remember it as if it were yesterday. I was the one who had to chase away the flies from his face.

My mother breastfed all of us. All peasant women breastfed their children for as long as they could, until they were two years old or more. I remember a three-year-old child called Gigi who lived at Le Muricce, a farm nearby: in the evening I used to hear him calling his mother who was working in the fields, 'Mummy, I want my milk!' If a mother had no milk she would either buy a nanny goat or look for a wet-nurse. My mother had plenty of milk and she often breastfed other people's children in order to earn a bit of money. Once she breastfed the son of a neighbour, and when the child grew up and got married, she breastfed his baby son Brunero too, as his wife had died in childbirth.

My father's name was Sabatino. *Sabato* means Saturday, so he must have been born on that day. He was short and sturdy. I adored him and followed him everywhere, and he was not strict with me because I was the smallest. But he didn't play with me. It wasn't the custom and it was considered a waste of time. My mother didn't play with me either. She was the *massaia*, that is to say she was responsible for the running of the house: she cooked all the meals, made the clothes and bedding, looked after the poultry and the rabbits, baked the bread, did the washing and made the *pecorino*, the sheep's cheese (when it was in season). My father was the *capoccia*, the head of the family, and was responsible for the farmwork, but in the house it was my mother who was in charge. She couldn't read, but even if she had been able to she wouldn't have had the time, and there wasn't the money to buy books. But my father had learnt to read and write when he was in the army. He could do sums, too, but so slowly and with such big numbers that to write down the price of a pig took him almost ten minutes.

My father was a good, hard-working man, but he wasn't very religious. He went to Mass only because our *padrone* insisted on it. Once the priest of Mercatale was preaching the sermon and he said, 'We must all tighten our belts!' When my father came home he told us about it and said, 'I'd like to have told that rascal that I hoped his throat would shrink, then he would eat less!' My father had once worked for that priest and knew he enjoyed his food. Later that priest got cancer of the throat and died, but my father didn't repent his words.

When I was small I had no one to play with because I was by far the youngest: my brother Azeglio was twenty years older than I was, and my youngest sister, Azeglia, was six years older. She was already a young lady and didn't want to play with me. So I stayed close to my parents, either in the field with my father or in the kitchen with my mother. Perhaps that is why I was able to cook years later.

In those days the children of farmers didn't have any toys. If my parents wanted to give me a present they gave me something to eat, like a dried fig or an orange. Our diet was monotonous, so we appreciated such treats very much. My most precious memories are of when the family sat round the fire in the evenings. The women would spin, the men would mend their tools, and then somebody would tell a story. My favourite stories were about *Beltordo*. He was a cunning fellow who lived at the court of a king, but he wasn't like the others who licked their master's boots. No, not he! In fact, when the King said to him, 'Look at all these people round me!' Beltordo said, 'Yes, they're like ants swarming round a service tree – to eat its bark!' For when he talked to the King he always had a ready answer and had no respect for his master. Once the King asked him, 'What is the saddest flower?'

'The one you find in a barrel!' said Beltordo at once. At the bottom of a wine cask you find a whitish material that looks like flour, so that when you see it you know the cask is nearly empty, and that's certainly a sad state of affairs!

The King was irritated because Beltordo always got the better of him, so one day he said: 'I don't want to see you again, either dressed or naked!' So Beltordo left the palace and returned wrapped in a fisherman's net.

In the end the King couldn't stand it any longer and he said to Beltordo, 'I'm going to have you hanged!'

'As you say, Sire, but at least grant me my last wish: to choose the tree you are going to hang me on.'

Unwisely, the King consented. Then Beltordo toured all the woods of the kingdom, but search as he might, he couldn't find a

Il Casino del Monte, the house where Pietro was born.

tree that suited him. Either they were too tall, or they were too small, or they had too many leaves, or they didn't have enough, or they were stunted or their branches were too thin. There was always something wrong with them. After many days' wandering he went back to the King and said, 'I'm sorry, Sire, but there is no tree in your kingdom which is to my liking, so you cannot have me hanged.' And so the King had to go on putting up with the impudent Beltordo.

These stories always made me laugh, even though I had heard them a hundred times. Naturally we were all on Beltordo's side and we were happy when he got the better of the King. Now I come to think of it, he was like a *mezzadro* and the King was like our *padrone*: we would like to have answered our *padrone* back like Beltordo did with the King, but we didn't dare to. We could only dream of doing it.

Another of my favourite stories was about Stoppa, a bandit who lived in the Maremma. My father would often tell me about him because his father used to take him food and in return he would receive a *marenghino d'oro*, a gold coin. Stoppa lived in a hut in the middle of a wood called the Macchia di Calandrone. He was so dangerous that even the *carabinieri* were afraid of him and didn't dare go near the place. Stoppa used to kidnap people and then ask their families for a ransom. One day he kidnapped a landowner and as usual sent a message to the man's family in order to organize the payment. The landowner's nephew presented himself at the agreed place and found Stoppa waiting for him. The bandit said, 'If you want your uncle back tomorrow you must bring me fifteen hundred gold coins.' The nephew replied, 'I'll bring you the money, but how do I know that you haven't killed him already?' Stoppa replied, 'Can you see that tree on top of that hill over there? Look well, your uncle is sitting up there beside it, you can see he's smoking a pipe. I'll give him back to you tomorrow.' So the nephew went home and returned to the same place the following day with a bag of coins. Stoppa took the bag, checked that the money was all there and said, 'All right, now you can go and reclaim your uncle.' Then he vanished. But when the nephew reached the top of the hill he found his uncle sitting on a chair with a pipe in his mouth, but he was dead. He had probably been dead the day before.

A few days ago I met a Florentine called Adami who has a holiday house in San Leolino. I happened to tell him how my grandfather had taken food to Stoppa, and I also told him about the man with the pipe. 'Goodness me!' said Florentine. 'The man with the pipe was an Adami, he was my grandfather!' What a coincidence. But my grandfather fared better than his, because mine received a gold coin, while his received a bullet in the heart.

We lived at Casino del Monte until I was nine years old, so I remember it well. It was on the edge of the forest and it had a beautiful view over the valley, though we didn't notice things like that then. The house was long and narrow, with a terrace at the top of the stairs where we used to eat during the summer. From there you entered the kitchen, which was a big room with two windows overlooking the *aia*, the threshing-floor. On the right there were two bedrooms, one for the boys and the other for the girls. When I was small not all my sisters were still living at home, otherwise the girls' bedroom would have been like a marketplace! On the left there were two bedrooms, one for my parents and the other for my uncle and his wife.

The stable for the oxen was on the ground floor, and next to it was the room where the chaff-cutting machine was kept (oxen have to have their hay chopped up small). In that room we kept the tools, too, spades and hoes and so on. Then there was the wine cellar, the room where we kept the sheep and the pigsty. Nearby was the barn: on the ground floor we kept the poplar leaves for the sheep, while on the first floor we stored the hay. The hay was for the oxen, though the sheep would have liked to eat it too. At the side of the house there was a valley with a stream running along it, and down there we had a vegetable garden. It was a cool place even in the summer, and there was always water in the stream for the vegetables. A thick hedge protected the garden from the sheep and pigs.

As at all farms we used a pond to water the animals, but we had to fetch drinking water for ourselves from a spring three hundred yards away down the hill. But after the spring at Nusenna this one seemed close by.

Casino del Monte was over half a mile from Mercatale, but we didn't feel isolated because people were constantly coming and going. The house stood beside a mule track that led to two villages higher up the hill, Sinciano and further still, Starda. What a strong wind blew at Sinciano when there was a *tramontana*! Up there was a *fattoria* with two families of *mezzadri* in the village and a few other *poderi* in the surrounding countryside. Although it was so high up it was not a poor *fattoria*, they had wheat, rye, vines, olive trees, sheep, pigs and plenty of *marroni* chestnuts. They were better off than at Montevarchi, where it was so foggy and damp in the winter and hot and humid in the summer. One of the farms belonged to the priest of Galatrona. He certainly had a lot of land. The main problem was the lack of water. There was a pond and some tanks for storing rainwater, but they had to go down to a fountain at Vie Piane, above Rendola, to get their drinking water. It was called Sinciano fountain but it was more than half a mile from the village and you know how much water weighs.

The village of Starda was more than two miles up the hill, under Montcluco. From there you could see Nusenna where my grandparents lived, but a deep valley lay in between. To go to my grandmother's shop the people of Starda had to walk through the woods. It was at least two miles away and all uphill or downhill. There was a *fattoria* at Starda too, it belonged to the Malaspina family. They say there was once a castle there – in fact there is a signpost indicating the Castle of Starda – but it must have fallen

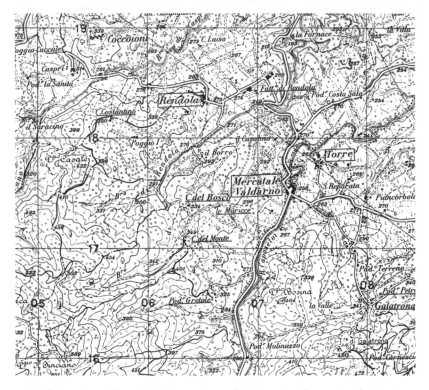

Military map showing Mercatale and its surroundings – underlined
are the places mentioned in the book.

into ruins a long time ago, because when I went as a child there
was just a huddle of houses on top of a little hill.

I remember a story about a girl who lived at Starda mill, down
by the stream. In those days there were no bathrooms, you used
to go into the woods to relieve yourself. She had some relations in
Montevarchi and when it was the town's feast day they invited
her to stay. They had a flushing toilet in their house, a novelty for
us country people. The toilet itself intimidated her, as well as all

30

those gleaming tiles. She felt so embarrassed in such an elegant place that she didn't manage to use the toilet at all. In the end they had to take her out into the country, otherwise she would have burst her bladder. I quite understand her because I had the same problem myself. One day my sister took me to San Giovanni to have my photograph taken, and at the studio there was a flushing toilet too. When I used it I felt ashamed because as soon as I flushed it everyone could hear the noise and knew what I had just done. It was better in the woods, you could hide yourself, no one could see you and they couldn't hear if you happened to let out a fart.

In those days the people who lived at Sinciano and Starda used to walk down the mule-track beside Casino del Monte whenever they wanted to go to Mercatale or Montevarchi. They often walked ten miles to get to work or go to the market and then they had to walk the same distance back again, but they took it for granted: there was no other way to get there. In the summer they used to walk barefoot so that they wouldn't wear out their clogs. The road was better maintained in those days – even the carters used to use it. The woodcutters passed that way too to get to the woods. They didn't cut down the big trees, just the small ones, in order to make charcoal. Other people passed by to look for mushrooms, chestnuts, acorns. Most of these folk paid rent for their houses and had no land, so they had to seek out things to eat.

The houses of the peasants were isolated, and yet someone passed almost every day. There was the *madonnaio*, who sold little pictures of the Madonna and other worthless odds and ends. There was the pedlar with his wooden box of thimbles, pins, buckles and so on, everything a housewife might need. There were the chairmakers: they came from Friuli in the north of Italy. You could tell from their different clothing that they came from afar. They travelled in groups of three or four and mended your chairs or made new ones in exchange for a bed and a good meal. The tinker came by to mend your pots and pans. Tinkers were often gypsies, but they were good, hard-working folk, and would also entertain us in the village square with their music and dancing. They were not like another type of gypsy, the fortune-tellers, who would steal your chickens if they got a chance. Then there was the fellow who sold *renino*, the fine sand we used to clean our greasy plates. He used to dig it up at Loccano, a group of houses near Montevarchi, and push it from house to house in a wheelbarrow. I don't know what the man's name was, I just remember that someone would call out across the fields, 'Here's the *renino*!' A tinful of the stuff would cost a *soldo*, a five-cent coin. It was backbreaking work and brought in very little money, in fact you had to be pretty desperate to undertake such a job.

I began to go to primary school when I was seven years old. The school was at La Torre, a little village on the other side of Mercatale. I had to walk down to Le Muricce and then go down along a farm track as far as the Montevarchi road. Then I had to go down a steep hill to the stream where there was the mill, and up the other side. It was well over a mile, but if the stream was in flood I walked even further, as I had to pass near the church of Mercatale in order not to wade through the stream (later on the Fascists built a bridge across it).

There were two shifts at school, one in the morning and one in the afternoon. I was in the second shift, so in the winter I had to walk home in the dark. The school consisted of a big classroom and in the winter it was very cold because we had no heating. They put me in the bottom class, but we shared the room with the other class. The teacher had to teach both at the same time. On the first day the teacher made me sit at the back of the class because I was quite tall. This was an advantage because I was a long way from the teacher, who frightened me; but it was also where the dunces and the more unruly boys were made to sit.

They all made fun of me, even though I was a year older than them.

It was normal for the Mercatale children to make fun of the peasants' children like me. They felt they were superior, even though they did not belong to the bourgeoisie. There wasn't any in the village: there were shopkeepers, carters, the carpenter, the smith and the man who ran the post office, a few small landowners; but the real 'gentlemen' lived in Montevarchi. Nevertheless, these boys were bolder than the peasants' children and they felt obliged to make fun of us and cheat us in every way possible. Thieving was quite common. If you left something lying about you could be sure that somebody would pinch it. Once my father gave me twenty *centesimi* in order to buy him a cigar and that disappeared too.

I remember that our teacher was an elderly lady, or at least she seemed so to me. She was very strict and she would give us a cuff at the least provocation. It was not like now, when children make a din in class and nobody scolds them. In those days if you spoke out of turn the teacher would give you a rap over the knuckles with her cane. But she never hit me. I was too shy to cause any trouble. At first we had a single textbook with everything in it, sums, history, geography and so on. I don't remember much about what I studied. I don't think that I understood everything I heard. For example, when we studied history the teacher kept talking about 'Costantino'. Now, there is a house above Rendola called Costantino, and I used to think: but is it possible that all those important things happened up there? I hadn't understood that Costantino was a Roman emperor.

The *Duce* had proclaimed that the children belonging to big families could study free, but we still had to buy the textbook, and also an exercise book, a pen and a pencil – quite an expense for a family like ours. On each desk there was an inkwell and a piece of blotting paper. Our exercise book had a lot of little squares in it, and when we were learning to write we had to fill the squares

Class photograph dating from Pietro's time.

with *paletti,* or little stakes: first they had to be vertical, then horizontal and then diagonal. I had never held a pen in my hand before and I found it difficult to control. It wobbled about or dropped out of my hand. I was often in a state of panic because if you weren't careful a blob of ink would form at the end of the nib and then drop on to the page. With all the *paletti* the teacher made me do I could have staked out all the vineyards of Tuscany!

The teacher gave us homework but we had no proper light at home so I had to study by the light of an oil lamp. The whole family was present as the kitchen was the only room which had a fire in it, so it was difficult to concentrate.

I may not have picked up much knowledge that first year, but I did acquire one thing: a headful of lice. People in the village would delouse you for a small consideration: they would examine your hair strand by strand and when they found a louse they would squash it against their thumbnail. But it was quicker to go to the barber and have your hair shaved off. My mother would then smear my scalp with a foul-smelling lotion which made the lice take fright and run away. Actually, we boys often had our heads shaved in the summer anyway, as it was hard to clean our hair with soap. Shampoo didn't exist in those days.

I had to repeat my first year at school. Perhaps I was a bit slow, but I think it was because I was frightened of that strict teacher, and also of the other children who made fun of me. Now I attended the school in Mercatale, which was closer to my home, and I had to go only in the mornings. I stayed there for four years, and then my father died suddenly and I had to leave school to look after the pigs. But at that time nobody thought it was important to continue. In theory the first three years of school were compulsory, but many children did not attend regularly and some did not go at all. The teachers were probably relieved, as the classes were too large anyway, and, after all, what was the use of studying if you were going to work in the fields for the rest of your life? For most of us it was enough to be able to read and write a little, sign our names, do sums. That was all. However, I am glad that I stayed at school until I was eleven, because at least I learnt to read quite well. Otherwise I wouldn't be able to read whole books as I do now. I can write too, though my spelling isn't all that good.

Although we didn't have toys in those days, we certainly played all sorts of games. We used the objects that came to hand: stones, coins, pebbles, pieces of wood. Either before school or after it we often played in the street or in the square of Mercatale. It was just earth in those days and there were no cars. If a cart came along you could hear it rumble a long distance away. One game was called *smuriella*. The *smuriella* was a flat stone, and on it we put another stone called the *lussi*. Each player put a small coin on the *lussi*. Then we took turns at throwing stones from a fixed distance, trying to move the *lussi* and knock the coins off it. If the player managed to knock the coins on to the ground he could pocket them, but not if they fell on to the *smuriella*. I don't think children play this game any more, but we still say, 'Today I've worked for the *lussi*,' that is, I've worked without earning anything.

Another game was called *bucarella*. We made nine little holes in the ground in rows of three, and then we each put a coin in the middle hole, which was called the *tosci*. Then we took a little metal ball and took turns to try and throw it into the *tosci*. Whoever succeeded could take all the coins, but if your ball fell into one of the other holes you could take only the coin you had put in yourself. Then there was *ribis*. The *ribis* was a piece of wood with two sharp ends, and the middle part was thicker, so when you put the *ribis* on the ground the two ends remained in the air. We used to draw a line in the ground with a stick and we would put a row of coins in it. Then we took turns to hit one of the ends of the *ribis* with the stick. It would jump into the air, and if it touched one of the coins it was yours.

The girls didn't play these games, they had games of their own. I remember they used to play hopscotch. Boys and girls never played together. If a boy had played with the girls the other boys would have made fun of him.

Now children have more sophisticated games, but I remember having a lot of fun with our simple ones. I also liked them very much because they gave me a chance to pass the time with other boys, even if they did pull my leg sometimes.

I went to school from 1934 to 1938, during the Fascist regime. In order to be able to send his children to school my father had to become a member of the Fascist party. It cost two lira, no small sum. All heads of family joined the party, otherwise you would get nowhere. But my father wasn't really a Fascist. He was nothing but a poor peasant and had to keep his mouth shut, that's all. When the teacher called out the register at school you had to say, 'Present', and make the Fascist salute. I found this difficult because at home we weren't Fascists and if we made the salute it was only to make fun of it, and my father didn't call Mussolini 'Duce' but 'that turkeycock at the head of the government'. At school they made us sing Fascist songs while we were doing gymnastics, but we didn't understand the words at all. Then we had Fascist sayings written in our textbook: 'Believe, Obey, Fight', 'Book and Gun, the Perfect Fascist', 'The Duce is always Right', and 'The Plough makes the Furrow but the Sword defends it', and so on (the Fascists loved capital letters, just as they loved uniforms and marches . . .). The young Fascists all went to meetings with a lot of fine speeches and took part in marches with flags a-flying and all that sort of nonsense, but I don't think they were real Fascists. They liked the uniforms and they thought it was a lot of fun. Certainly at the end of the war they weren't Fascists any more, only the fanatical ones remained and they got beaten up or worse.

I remember an episode that happened at school. I remember it so well because it caused me a lot of heartache. From time to time a school inspector came up from Montevarchi to see how our studies were going, and he used to set us a task. On this occasion he gave us a problem to solve: 'Students send the Duce photographs of beautiful new schools, but he would like to see photos of the dilapidated ones. Why?' I thought the answer was simple: he wanted to see photographs of the dilapidated ones because he wanted to make them beautiful. So I wrote this in my exercise book. But the other children didn't understand the question and wrote rubbish. When the teacher began to look at the exercise books she grew angry because she didn't want to be humiliated in front of the inspector. She took the exercise books one by one and slammed them down on the desk saying, 'This is wrong, and so's this one, and this one.' In the end she didn't even open them, but if she had looked at mine she would have seen I had written the right answer. She was furious, which was why I hadn't the courage to say anything. I wanted to tell her but I didn't dare, and this still rankles every time I think of it.

CHAPTER 2

At Work

One day the *padrone* called my father to his office. When my father returned he looked very depressed. It was summertime and we were eating on the terrace because it was cooler than in the house. The *padrone* had told him that we had to move from Casino del Monte to Casa del Bosco, and my father didn't know how to break the news to us, poor man. Casa del Bosco was only three hundred yards away, but nobody wanted to work the land there because the soil was very heavy and hard to plough. Also, you couldn't sow maize, and we needed maize for our poultry. Nor did it have a terrace like at Casino del Monte where we used to eat during the summer, and also hang up the maize, the tomatoes, the onions and so on.

The *padrone* wanted to put another family in Casino del Monte, a family with more males. At that time my uncles had both died and the only adult males were my father, my cousin Edoardo and my brother Azeglio: my sisters didn't count according to the *padrone*, though they were robust and worked in the fields too. But in order to move us to Casa del Bosco the *padrone* had to find an excuse to send away the family that was already living there. Soon he found one, a little aeroplane. At that time it was a custom to carve a little wooden aeroplane and put it on the top of the haystack or the barn. It served as a weathervane, which was very useful when you were winnowing, because if you didn't know from which direction the wind was blowing, all the dust would go into your eyes. So the farmer who lived at Casa del Bosco made a little aeroplane too and put it on top of his barn. Later on the *padrone* saw it and said: 'You ask me to find you workers to help you with the olive-pruning, but I see that you waste your time with useless things like that!' He pointed at the little aeroplane and with his next words ordered the poor farmer to leave the farm.

Nowadays we can't imagine a thing like that happening, but in those days we took it for granted, not without grumbling, of course. The *padrone* was boss and the peasant had to submit to his will. I remember another case: my *padrone* sent a peasant away from his farm because the latter had bought a pocket watch with a chain. He had been doing his military service and no doubt he had saved up the little money he had received. But in those days only the *padrone* had a pocket watch. Evidently he considered that he was the only one who had the right to know the time.

Have you seen the film *The Tree of Clogs*, which describes the life of a peasant family in Emilia-Romagna, north-east of Tuscany? In the film a little boy's clogs were worn out, so his father secretly cut down a small poplar tree with which to make him another pair; otherwise the boy would have had to go barefoot and it was still wintertime. But the bailiff saw the trunk that had been sawn off, and as bailiffs will he told the *padrone* what the peasant had done. So the *padrone* sent the peasant and his family away from the farm: all because of a piece of wood. But that peasant wasn't very crafty! If you want to steal a tree you must cut it flush with the ground and cover the stump with moss and dry leaves. In that way nothing can be seen, I know because I've done it dozens of times. It seems to me that the peasants in Emilia-Romagna are not so cunning as the Tuscans!

You may wonder what one had to do to get permission to cut down a tree. You had to ask the woodsman, the man who looked after the woods on the *padrone*'s property. Even if you simply needed to make a handle for a hayfork or a hoe, tools that you used on the land. But he didn't give his permission free, don't you worry! You had to give him a flask of wine or a bottle of olive oil. Oh yes, there was the Mafia in those days as well, if you wanted a favour you had to pay in kind.

We were also unwilling to go and live in Casa del Bosco because of the family who lived there, the Cini, who were a miserable, squalid lot. The head of the family was an old woman who was said to be a witch. She used to go around with a stick in one hand and a little earthenware pot in the other. It was said that in the pot there was some oil, and if you went close to her she would put her finger into it and try to smear you with it, in order to cast a spell on you. So everyone avoided her. Even after the family had left the house you could still actually smell the poverty and meanness. They were so miserly that they gave the children bread made out of bran, which was considered fit only for animals. The adults ate proper bread. The *padrone* discovered this when one of the family, Gino, an orphan adopted from the Ospedale degli Innocenti, went with his adoptive mother down to the olive press in Mercatale to take the head of the family his lunch. His mother put down the lunch basket and wanted to go home, but the little boy begged her to let him stay and eat with his father. 'Here I can eat white bread,' he explained to the company, 'while at home we have only bread made out of bran.' The *padrone*, ever vigilant, heard these words and said to the father: 'Aha, now I know why you are always asking for bran to give to your pigs!' Perhaps that was another reason for sending the family away from Casa del Bosco.

When the governors of the orphanage in Florence heard that the boy had been given bread made out of bran they sent someone to take the boy back. But he didn't want to go back to Florence, so he hid inside an empty olive oil jar, pulling the wooden lid over the top. Nobody could find him and the official went away. Gino told us about this later, when he came to work for my family during the war. The Cini went to live in a farm near the village of Cennina, and their descendants live there still.

So we resigned ourselves to our fate and went to live in Casa del Bosco. We didn't like it at first but then we got used to it. It had one advantage: the kitchen was on the ground floor, which was unusual in those days, so in order to feed the oxen you didn't have to go outside. You just had to walk through the room that held the chaff-cutter and into the stable. On the other side of the kitchen was the cellar, which faced north and was nice and cool. We had to go outside only to feed the sheep – their stable had a separate door opening on to the threshing-floor. The bedrooms were on the first floor. Mine was over the sheep's stable, and I could hear them bleating in the morning. I shared a bed with my brother Azeglio, while my cousin Edoardo slept in another one. My sisters slept in the next bedroom, but two of them had already left home: Marsiglia had gone to live as a maidservant with our *padrone* and Nunzia had married and gone to live in Florence.

La Casa del Bosco, the house where Pietro spent most of
his working life.

My sisters slept two or three to a bed, which was normal then. We were packed tight like anchovies in a barrel but at least we felt the cold less that way. My parents slept in the room over the kitchen. When my father died my mother didn't want to sleep there any more, so it became a sort of storeroom, and we used to hang the salamis and hams there because the chimney of the kitchen fireplace was inside one of the walls. My mother went to sleep with her daughters, Silvia and Azeglia.

On the first floor was a room where we stored the grain and kept the silkworms. And the sitting room was up there too. It had a table, a few chairs and a cupboard with a glass front. We had no armchairs, only rich people had those. On public holidays we used to take guests upstairs to drink a glass of *vinsanto*. But otherwise we would stay in the kitchen where it was warmer. The fire was kept burning all day long.

Behind the house stood a barn. We used to keep the hay, the wheat husks and the poplar leaves here. We pruned the poplar trees in summer and gave the leaves to the sheep during the winter. When we pruned the olive trees we tied up the prunings in bundles and kept those in the barn too. When summer came we would beat the leaves off and put them aside for the winter. Winters were long in those days and we had to feed the animals with what little we had.

In 1938 I began the school year with plenty of ambition and will to study. The government said they would help big families. A family with five children was considered big, so a family like ours, with eight children, deserved extra help. My sisters had already stopped going to school, so they amused themselves making plans for my future. 'Become a lawyer,' said one. 'Then you will be deceived by nobody.' 'No, you'd better be a bailiff,' said another. 'Then the *padrone* will listen to your words.' My mother wanted me to be a doctor, to save on doctors' bills and medicines.

And what about me? I wanted to study history and become a professor. But I held my tongue because I knew my family wanted me to study something that would serve them in the future. In their opinion history was completely useless.

But all my dreams went up in smoke because my father sud-

Sabatino, Pietro's father.

denly had a stroke and died. I was eleven at the time and was in bed with influenza. I heard my mother call up the stairs, 'Sabo, Sabo,' as she did every morning. He got up, sat on the chair to put on his clogs and died on the spot. He was not old, he was only fifty-four. When I heard what had happened I thought I was having a bad dream. I didn't want to admit to myself that he was dead, I wanted things to go on as they had gone before. Then there was the funeral, but I was still confined to my bed.

After all the grieving and the upheaval my father's death caused, life had to go on, farmwork cannot wait. The day after the funeral my cousin Edoardo was summoned to the *padrone*'s office. He was now head of the family and responsible for the farm. It was then that the *padrone* told him that I would have to leave school in order to look after the pigs. One of my sisters would then be free to work in the fields.

Words can't describe how disappointed I was. Not studying meant a life of virtual slavery, the life that my father had led. I couldn't study history in the woods! Anyhow, my family fitted me out with a new pair of clogs and that November, aged eleven, I began my life as a swineherd. I had to drive the pigs into the woods beneath the house for several hours every morning, and then again in the afternoon. I took them under the oak trees so that they could eat the acorns. I sometimes took them a long way up the hill, as far as the Sinciano fountain at Vie Piane. In the summer I would take them down to the stream, because pigs suffer from the heat and they liked to roll in the water and the mud to cool themselves down. Usually I was alone, but sometimes I met up with other lads with their pigs, and then we would let the animals rootle together under the trees so that we could chat or play some game. I remember that we made a sort of bowling green down by the stream, but that our balls didn't run very straight because we had shaped them with our billhooks.

I had to go into the woods with the pigs every day, even when the weather was bad. If it was very cold my mother would give me a couple of matches inside a box so that I could light a fire. Try lighting a fire with damp wood and only two matches!

When we took pigs or sheep into the woods we had to be careful to respect the boundaries. To make sure we made no mistakes there were the gamewardens and the *guardie campestri* prowling around. They were not very popular with the peasants because they kept us under observation and would run to the *padrone* if they found us doing something wrong. If a pig or a sheep crossed the boundary between one property and another, one of the wardens would tell the head of the family, and we had to give him a present, a flask of olive oil, a chicken or a dozen eggs, otherwise the *padrone* would be informed of the transgression. These wardens were nothing better than spies, the villains. At least, we thought of them as villains, but after all they were poorly paid and victims of the whole system too and had children to rear just like anybody else.

So I began to go to the woods every day and bit by bit I came to know every stream, every chestnut grove, every little valley, like the palm of my hand. Even now when Guido, my *padrone*'s heir, wants to check the boundaries he calls me, because I am one of the few people left who know them well. When I was a boy the Bigoli family – for this was my *padrone*'s surname – owned little scraps of land scattered all over the woods, a hectare here, a hectare there. There's a long story behind this. A century or so ago, nobody knows exactly when, Torello, a member of the Bigoli family, became a priest. When people were on their deathbeds he would go to hear them confess before administering the last rites, as is still the custom. Well, there's no one in this world who hasn't done wrong in one way or another. When Torello listened to people's confessions his eyes would begin to bulge with alarm, then he would wring his hands and cross himself. 'These are sins,' he would declare, 'that God will never be able to pardon! You will be damned and sent to hell, there's no doubt about that!' The dying man would then begin to weep and moan, and between one sob and another he would ask the priest what he must do to avoid such a fate. The priest replied at once: 'You must leave some land to the Church, and then you will see that God will forgive even the gravest of sins.' So the dying man would hurriedly make his will with the help of the priest. But as he didn't know how to read and write he didn't realize that the priest was assigning the piece of land to his own family, the Bigolis, and not to the Church at all.

Finally the priest himself died, and the truth came out: Torello, a priest, had stolen from the Holy Church! It was a great scandal, and for months it was the main topic of conversation in Mercatale. After the funeral Torello was buried in the Bigoli family's private chapel in the cemetery. But then the rumour began that every morning he was found moaning up on the roof. It must have been his soul, as his body was confined in the coffin. People said he moaned because he did not feel at ease in the cemetery, damned as he was. So they called one of the Capuchin monks from the monastery at Montevarchi to deal with the problem. 'He is suffering because he can hear the church bells,' said the monk. 'They trouble him because he is damned. We must take him to a place where he can hear them no longer.' So they took the coffin out of the ground, the monk uttered a few prayers, and then four strong men hoisted it on to their shoulders and began to walk towards the hills, followed by the monk. They passed Casino del Monte and made their way in the direction of Sinciano. 'My God, how heavy he is,' the four men groaned, so the monk said they must carry the coffin still further. It must indeed have been heavy, because in those days coffins were made of planks that had been hewn by hand with an axe and so were very thick. They didn't have electric saws in those days. Then, as you know, if you are carrying something heavy uphill, it seems to get heavier and heavier with every step you take. Anyway, at last they reached Vie Piane, and the path began to go downhill into a narrow valley where Torello had a piece of woodland. I suppose he stole that too. 'Now he weighs less,' said the men, relieved. 'Here he will no longer hear the church bells,' said the monk. 'You can bury him in this valley.' And so they did.

The real name of that valley was Borro della Vecchia, the Valley of the Old Woman, but from then on it was called Borro di Torello. And if a cold wind blew from that direction people used to say it was Torello's fault. If a hailstorm came, it was his fault too. Once one of the gamewardens was near that valley and he saw a blackbird in a bush. He aimed and shot, but the blackbird flew away. He shot again and again the blackbird escaped. 'Why is this?' said the gamewarden and took another shot. The blackbird flew away a third time and the man was about to follow him when he had a thought. 'I am in Torello's valley, perhaps this blackbird is Torello in disguise. After all, he wore black when he was alive.' He stood for a moment paralysed with terror, and then ran away as fast as his legs would carry him.

So that is the story about Torello. Who knows whether it is true? I didn't really believe it, but when I was in the woods with the pigs I used to look for the tomb: people said that there was a gravestone with four little columns. But I never found it. Perhaps it was covered up by brambles, perhaps it had never existed. But the fact remains that the heirs of the Bigoli family still own at least ten small pieces of woodland scattered all over these hills. Now they are covered with dense undergrowth, but in those days they were worth a good deal. You could gather *marroni* there and acorns and plenty of wood to make charcoal with. If the story about Torello is true it explains why there are all these little pieces of land. Then there is the old folk's home at Bucine. After Torello's death one of his nephews became a priest too. He seems to have had a guilty conscience because when he died he did not leave his share of the family wealth to his family, but gave instructions that the money should be used to build the home at Bucine, near his parish. Perhaps he wanted to ask God's pardon for the sins of his uncle.

But this is not the end of the story. On one side of the square in

Mercatale were the storehouses owned by my *padrone*, who was the last of the Bigoli family. On the first floor there was a bedroom with the door ajar which everyone said belonged to Torello. When the olive press was in action the *frantoiano*, the man responsible for the production of the oil, used to sleep there. He said that during the night Torello used to come in and snatch the blankets off his bed. Sometimes he would hear him harnessing his horse in the stable below. So nobody else dared enter that room. They were afraid they might find Torello there. The truth came out later: it appears that the *frantoiano* used to steal a bit of oil from the *padrone* and he hid it in that room, which is why he told those stories.

My *padrone* died in 1962 and his heirs planned to come to Mercatale to share out his possessions. So I said to myself, 'Let's have a look before they come, I may find something useful.' That night I went into Torello's room. As you can imagine it was a mass of cobwebs, but there was a fine wrought-iron bed in the middle of the room. A straw mattress had been on it but there was only a handful of dust left. It must have been eaten by rats. I removed the bed, the table and the wardrobe, making several journeys during the night. Nobody knew they were there. You can't call it stealing if the owners didn't know they possessed those things in the first place, can you? And nobody would have wanted Torello's bed, anyway. Now Jenny sleeps in it but nobody pulls her bedclothes off.

Back in the 1930s our *padrone* was, unfortunately, still very much alive, and the life we *mezzadri* lived under his thumb was a hard one, though we took it for granted at the time.

We used to get up early, as soon as the sun rose, or even earlier. If the weather was warm we would open the shutters, otherwise we would keep them shut because there was no glass in the windows – only rich people had that. Then we would go outside to relieve ourselves. We didn't wash, but we would splash our faces with water from a pitcher on the sink in the kitchen. To clean our teeth we would rub them with sage leaves when they were in season, but often we didn't clean them at all. There was no toothpaste then, or if there was we couldn't have afforded it, anyway. When our hands were very dirty we used to clean them with a stone. We would choose a smooth one from the stream and rub our hands with it, our feet too if they were very dirty. In the summer the younger members of the family would bathe in the stream, but during the winter we never washed our bodies. Probably we smelt, but we didn't notice it ourselves. Perhaps we were used to the smell. It may be that some of the dirt attached itself to our clothes, and my mother did wash our clothes from time to time. On the rare occasions that we used soap we found that it got into our eyes, and we were afraid of blinding ourselves. The stone was better. I don't remember ever washing my hair, perhaps some of the dirt came out when we bathed in the stream.

To wash our clothes my mother put them all into a big earthenware *conca*, a kind of pot with a diameter at waist height of about three feet. It had a hole at the bottom, so she put an earthenware plate underneath it. She covered the clothes with a piece of cloth, and then she took some wood ash from the fireplace and laid it over the cloth. Meanwhile she had heated some water in the cauldron over the fire and now she ladled the boiling water over the ash. The water filtered through the clothes on to the plate, whereupon my mother would ladle it back into the cauldron, reheat it and pour it again on to the ash. She did this three or four times, and then she left the clothes in the *conca* overnight. In the morning my father harnessed the oxen to the cart, put the clothes on to it and took them down to the stream. There my mother would rub and beat the clothes on the stones beside the stream until they were clean. Then they would carry the clothes home on the cart and my mother would hang them out to dry on the line. When they were dry she folded them carefully and put them away in the wardrobe. She never ironed them – we didn't even possess an iron – but, after all, we never went to parties, so it didn't matter if our clothes were a bit crumpled.

All our clothes were made at home. To make socks and shirts for the winter we used wool from our sheep. We sheared them in the spring, round about March. Then one of the women took a flange of wool and wrapped it round a distaff, a kind of stick with a thickened end. She held the distaff with one hand and with the other she pulled the wool out and put it on a spindle. Then she made a skein, and finally a ball of wool was ready for knitting, but I won't explain all the details because you'll never have to do it. I assure you, however, that a lot of skill was required. It was considered to be a woman's job. I've never seen a man spin – it would have been a ridiculous sight.

The women used to spin whenever they could find the time, even when they were looking after the pigs or the sheep, but particularly after supper when we were all sitting round the fire in the kitchen. They had to spin a great deal of the time because clothes had to be made for the whole family, and families were numerous in those days. Each woman had to spin a certain amount of wool every week. I hope they weren't all like the girl in the rhyme:

Lunedì lunediài!	Monday, Monday, oh dear!
Martedì mi riposai.	On Tuesday I had a rest.
Mercoledì persi la rocca,	On Wednesday I lost my distaff,
Giovedì la ritrovai.	On Thursday I found it again.
Venerdì la inconocchiai.	On Friday I prepared the distaff,
Sabato mi lavai la testa,	On Saturday I washed my hair,
Domenica non lavorai perché era festa!	On Sunday I didn't work because it was a holiday!

The women used to spin hemp too, a plant we grew in the garden. When the stalks were about six feet tall we used to cut them down and spread them in the sun to dry. Then we would

Girl spinning with distaff.

soak them in the pond. When they were well softened we would lift them out and comb them to separate the strands, and then the women would spin them in the same way as the wool.

When the women had finished spinning the wool and the hemp, they would carry the balls to some peasant's wife who had a loom. The women with looms often had some physical handicap, so that they couldn't work in the fields. I remember there was a loom at Casino del Monte. It was in the sheep's stable, so you can imagine how much dirt got woven into the cloth! The woman used either to weave wool by itself, or mix it with hemp. As payment she took a bit of the cloth, because nobody had any money to pay her with.

When the cloth was ready my mother used to carry it home and make our clothes with it. She used a pattern, various pieces of paper that she used to pin on to the cloth, and then she would cut round them. Then she would sew the pieces together. I don't think she was a skilled sempstress, but what did it matter if the clothes weren't perfectly styled? We were only going to wear them in the fields. I remember that the shirts made of wool and hemp used to scratch you when they were new. As for the sheets they were like cheese graters, but after a few washings they would soften up. She had to knit our socks and jumpers herself, so her hands were never idle, even after supper when we sat round the fire.

When I was a child the fire on the kitchen hearth was all we had to heat the house and to cook on. My mother used to light the fire even in the summer. I remember how the poor woman used to sweat when she bent over the fire to stir the soup. Then the fire was too hot, but in the winter it was never hot enough. It burnt your face but your buttocks were still freezing cold. Now and then you had to turn yourself round, just like when you turn the meat round when you are frying it in the pan. On the sides of the fireplace were two holes with an iron grill over them: my mother used to put embers there to cook food slowly or to keep it warm. On the lower part of the hearth was a kind of drawer where my mother used to put clothes or sheets to take the damp out of them.

We didn't use the fire to make breakfast because we always ate cold food, but only after we had fed the oxen and the other animals. We wouldn't have enjoyed our meal if they had been hungry. We used to eat bread and *companatico*, something to go with the bread which varied according to the season: a piece of bacon, an onion, a clove of garlic, raw broad beans, some fruit, a handful of chestnuts, whatever was available. We often ate *a pinzimonio*, dipping raw vegetables into olive oil to which salt and pepper have been added.

Con olio, aceto, pepe e sale	With olive oil, vinegar, salt and pepper
Sarebbe buon uno stivale.	Even a boot would taste good.

For lunch we almost always had *zuppa di pane*, soup with bread in it, which my mother had prepared in a pot hanging over the fire. She would put all sorts of things into it: beans, black cabbage, onions, potatoes, whatever was in season, and she would add some plants that grew wild in the fields too. We would have only one course. When we ate fruit we would pick it directly from the tree and eat it on the spot: cherries, apples, pears, peaches, figs – there was plenty of everything. We would have *zuppa di pane* in the evening as well, or bean soup, at any rate a soup of some kind. People said it was easy to digest in the evening. It certainly made you feel full, for a few hours, anyway. We didn't eat much meat but we used to eat a lot of beans, which nowadays they say make a good substitute. A family living near Mercatale used to get through sixty *staia* of beans in a year. A *staio* contained nineteen kilos, so there must have been a lot of farting going on in that household!

We used to eat meat only on Sundays. My mother would kill a chicken, a rabbit or a duck. She would stew it over the fire, and use the gravy as a sauce for the pasta. She would make *tagliatelle* and *maccheroni* by hand, she never dreamt of buying ready-made pasta. In the evening we would eat the meat with some potatoes. Sometimes she would fry some pieces of rabbit, and some courgette flowers, if they were in season. But not often, because frying used up too much oil. Sometimes we would eat fish: either we bought a bit of dried stockfish, or my brother would catch some minnows or freshwater crabs down by the stream. In the summer my mother made *panzanella* with stale bread that had been soaked in water, tomatoes, onions, basil and a little oil and vinegar. We would eat sheep's cheese only when we were in the fields. When we were mowing the hay, for example, we didn't want to waste time going into the house for lunch, so we would eat bread and cheese and a handful of broad beans, or perhaps salami or ham. We would wash all this down with wine, but we would add water to it to make it last longer.

When I was a child my mother bought very little food. A little bit of *grandinina* perhaps, to put in our soup, some rice, some chestnut flour, or some maize flour to make polenta with. At harvest-time she bought tunnyfish and anchovies to give the men more energy for all that hard work. But we had little money to spend and usually she had to manage with what grew on the farm. And she managed very well because there was always food on the table and I don't remember ever suffering from hunger. If people nowadays ate as we did perhaps they would be more healthy. The food was genuine too, as we didn't put poisons on to the fields or give factory-made meal to our animals, and if an apple had a slight bruise we would just eat round it. We didn't throw the whole apple away like people do now.

Nor did we buy bread, we made it at home. I used to help my mother to make it when I was quite small, so that when I was older I was able to make bread all by myself. Every Saturday we put the flour into the *madia*, poured on to it the right amount of water and kneaded it well, and then we added a bit of yeast, which was in a piece of dough we had left from the week before. While the dough was 'resting' we would heat the oven in the wall just outside the front door with bundles of tree heather or vine-prunings. We would put something specially tasty in with the bread, like a bun with grapes in it. We made fifteen loaves at a time, because they had to last the whole week and we ate bread in large quantities. Once a month we would take three or four sacks of grain down to the mill to have it ground into flour. We couldn't store much flour in the house because it would turn mouldy very quickly. We brought the bran back from the mill too, to give to the pigs. It makes me laugh when I see bran for sale in the chemist's shop: when I was young it was considered fit only for animals and it was consequently much cheaper.

After supper the family would sit round the fire, especially in the winter when it got dark early so we couldn't work outside. Before we went to bed my mother prepared a *prete* or 'priest' for each bed: this was a wooden framework inside which you hooked a little metal pot full of embers from the fire. This sign of disrespect for those in holy orders was quite common, I'm afraid! She would cover the embers with ash so that there would be no sparks and then she would put one in each bed to warm it. Before getting into bed we would remove the priest and put it outside the bedroom door. The rooms may have been icy but thanks to the priest it was wonderfully cosy in bed. The mattresses were stuffed with maize leaves, only rich people had mattresses stuffed with feathers. Ours were full of lumps but we slept well all the same.

Before the war we had no electricity in the house. The fire gave a bit of light and sometimes we would use paraffin lamps. To light the way to bed we would use olive oil lamps, which we hung along the chimney mantelpiece. They gave little light, all we needed to take the priest out and get into bed. We didn't undress, we just took off our clogs. Then we would put the lamp out

Concetta, Pietro's mother.

immediately to save the oil. I often went to bed without a lamp, as there were not enough of them to go round. I could climb the stairs, go into my bedroom, take off my shoes and get into bed, all in pitch darkness. If I should ever go blind I could manage perfectly well.

That reminds me of a story. A farmer had an ox with a swollen leg so he called the vet. In those days vets weren't scientific like they are now. This one told the farmer to fry some earthworms in olive oil and use them to make poultices for the swelling: he was to apply one poultice in the evening and one the following morning. So the farmer went out to the manure heap and dug up some nice juicy worms, and then he fried them. After making the first poultice he didn't know where to put the remaining worms. 'Give them to me,' said his wife, 'I'll put them on a plate and hide them in the *madia*, otherwise the cats will get them.' And that is what she did.

The farmer's son had gone out to spend the evening with some friends and when he came back he was ravenous. He went to the *madia* to look for something to eat, but as it was dark and he had no lamp he couldn't see what was inside. Groping around inside he found the plate of worms and, propping the *madia* lid on his head, he broke off a piece of bread and used it to scoop up the worms into his mouth. Then he went to bed.

The next morning the farmer's wife looked for the worms in the *madia* but couldn't find them. 'Did you take that stuff for the poultice?' she shouted to her husband who was in the stable. Her son was still in bed but he heard her shout. 'If you mean that stuff on a plate in the *madia*, I ate it last night. What was it? It certainly tasted good!'

Many years later it was the fashion to rear earthworms in order to make humus. They were talking about it in the bar in Mercatale and somebody said that these earthworms were also good to eat. 'We know that already,' said another. 'Ask Quirino, he ate a plateful when he was a lad!'

57

Those earthworms certainly didn't do Quirino any harm, even though they had come from the manure-heap, because he is now ninety-two and lively as a cricket.

Yes, we were certainly very poor, I realize that now. But we accepted our condition, all the other peasants were equally poor and we didn't expect anything else from life. We bought almost nothing, partly because we didn't need to and partly because we had very little money anyway. Sometimes we resorted to barter: for example, if the smith mended our plough we would give him a flask of wine. The only things we had to buy for the house were matches and salt. In fact, if you saw a peasant looking worried, you'd ask, '*A che cosa pensi, ai quattrini del sale?*' 'What are you worried about, money for salt?' Because salt was essential for the preparation of ham and salamis.

When my father died my cousin Edoardo became *capoccia*, and it was he who had to do the accounts with the *padrone*. At the end of December he would go to the farm office to meet the *padrone* and the administrator. They had to calculate how much the farm had earned during the year: how much wine and oil had been sold, how many pigs and lambs, how many calves and so on. Then they subtracted the expenses and divided what was left. The small sum that the farmer received had to be enough to keep the family for the rest of the year.

Fortunately our *padrone*, for all his faults, was scrupulously honest when it came to dividing the profits. He never gave away a *centesimo*, but neither did he steal one. The profits were not always shared out so fairly. On the big *fattorie* it was not usually the landowner who cheated but the farm bailiff, and what he subtracted he put into his own pocket, his master knew nothing about it. But the *padrone* could be unfair in other respects: if there had been a good harvest he would say it was thanks to the fine weather, while if the harvest was bad he would always blame the wretched farmer.

Sometimes the *padrone* would give the peasant some eggs and the farmer would provide a broody hen to sit on them. But if he gave you twenty eggs he wanted twenty chicks. It often happens that not all the eggs hatch and even if they do the chicks may die when they are small. Either they fall into the pond and get drowned or a cat gobbles them up when their mother is not looking, and so on. So we used to repeat the old rhyme:

Padrone, andrà bene questa chiocciata?	Master, will this clutch of chicks be all right?
Di ventun uova mi è nato un pulcino,	Only one egg hatched out of twenty-one,
Il pulcino è morto, la chioccia è malata,	The chick died, the hen is sick,
Padrone, andrà bene questa chiocciata?	Master, will this clutch of chicks be all right?

Every peasant knew this rhyme and would repeat it even if, for example, a hailstorm destroyed the grapes: 'Master, will this clutch of chicks be all right?' He knew that the *padrone* would blame him anyway.

Certainly the *padrone* always had the upper hand. When a peasant went to live on a farm the *padrone* would read him the terms of the agreement. Now, I believe that when two people come to an agreement they should also agree on the conditions. But it was always the *padrone* who made the decisions, otherwise he wouldn't hand over the farm. Everything had to be paid for in kind: for example, when the grain was weighed and shared out the farmer had to give the *padrone* a couple of chickens. Another couple when the wine was drawn off. At Christmas he wanted a couple of capons, and they had to be ready for the table.

This reminds me of something that happened to Boccio, a friend of mine. On Christmas Eve he took the train to Florence, carrying the presents he had to give to the *padrone*: two fat capons and a broom made of broomcorn. When he reached Florence he got off the train and began to look about him, not quite remembering which way to go and being too shy to ask anyone. Around

Christmas a lot of peasants used to take presents to their *padroni* and the cunning Florentines would hang round the station to see if they could in some devious way get hold of the gifts. In fact, that's what happened to our poor Boccio: a Florentine saw him standing there looking lost and immediately went up to him. 'Good morning,' he said, 'the *padrone* sent me to meet you.' 'That's kind of him,' said Boccio, without asking himself how the *padrone* had known he was coming when he hadn't been advised of the fact. 'And how is he?' 'He's in fine health,' said the Florentine. 'He's anxious to see you, so let's get going. I'll lead the way. I'll give you a hand if you like, give me those heavy capons and you can carry the broom.' After a few minutes' walking the Florentine stopped outside a cobbler's and said, 'Wait here, please, the *padrone* asked me to pick up some shoes he is having repaired.' He disappeared into the shop and Boccio stood waiting outside. But the other fellow didn't appear again. Finally the peasant plucked up courage and went into the shop. 'Did you see someone who came in to pick up a pair of shoes?' he asked the cobbler. 'A fellow carrying a couple of capons came in ten minutes ago,' replied the cobbler. 'But he didn't mention any shoes and he went out of the other door.' So poor Boccio was robbed of his capons, and when he finally found his *padrone*'s house he had only a broom to give him, for which he no doubt got the rough side of his master's tongue.

Certainly we were all in awe of the *padrone*, especially the young ones. We considered him a sort of monster, hardly a human being at all. I remember once one of my sisters ran into the house in a great state of excitement. She began to laugh and then to cry, saying, 'You wouldn't believe what I've seen, you wouldn't believe it!' Then it came out that she'd seen the *padrone* relieving himself in a field. She couldn't imagine that he had to pass water just like anyone else.

Among ourselves we called our *padrone* 'Groppa Secca' –

Skinnyrump – but his real name was Giuseppe Bigoli. He was tall and thin with the face of a scarecrow. He always went round with patches on his trousers and he wore a moth-eaten overcoat, to make people think he was poor. But when he died they discovered that he was the richest man in Mercatale: in the thirties he had had fifteen million lire in the bank. The bank was *Monte de' Paschi di Siena* and people used to say that the governors of the bank didn't want any more of his money because otherwise he could take the bank over. In the thirties fifteen million lire was an enormous sum, equivalent to a thousand million today. In those days a workman would earn five or six lire a day, not more. Of course, Groppa Secca's money devalued over the years, but he was a rich man right up to his death, even though he looked like a tramp.

With all that money Groppa Secca could have modernized his farms and he would still have been a rich man. But he never dreamed of doing that. He preferred us to live in those wretched conditions, so that all we thought of was making ends meet. Most of the small landowners were the same. They were called the *'padronelli'* (the little *padroni*), and they were careful to keep their farmers in a state of submission because they lived in close contact with them and socially there was not much gap between them. The important landowners, like the owners of the estates of Rendola and Petrolo, had little to do with the peasants, because they visited their lands only occasionally and left everything in the hands of the farm bailiff.

In the thirties Groppa Secca was the richest of the local *padronelli* and he could have afforded a bailiff too, but he didn't hire one, probably to avoid paying the man's salary. So he used to supervise us himself. He was present when we were ploughing or sowing, when we were scything the corn or harvesting it, when we picked the grapes or drew off the wine, when we gathered the olives or made the oil at the olive press. Whatever we were doing he would always turn up, wearing that worn and filthy overcoat. Apparently he was afraid that we weren't working properly or that we might steal an ear of grain or a drop of wine or oil.

Groppa Secca overawed us all: with him you couldn't laugh or sing or crack a joke. It was worse than being in the army. If you did speak he would say immediately with that shrill voice that grated on your ears like a rasp: 'What did you say? What did you say?' He had heard you the first time, but he wanted you to repeat your words to see whether you said the same thing again. He kept a check on you all the time. During the winter months he came to watch you working, and then he would begin to rub his hands together and say, 'How cold it is! May I go and warm my hands in front of your fire?' You couldn't say no, so he would go into the kitchen and hold his hands in front of the fire for a second or two. But he wasn't really cold, he just wanted to see what wood you were burning, in case you had taken a log or two without his permission.

I don't believe that Groppa Secca was really devout, otherwise he wouldn't have behaved as he did. However, he always went to Mass on Sundays and wanted every head of the family to go too. In fact, when he read out the terms of agreement to a new peasant he would always end up saying, '. . . and here it is the custom to go to Mass every Sunday.' So the head of the family knew that if he didn't go to church he would be sent away from the farm. In the church at Mercatale Groppa Secca had his private bench near the door, so that he could check that all his peasants were keeping to the rules. If one of the heads of the family didn't turn up he would be summoned to the farm office the next day and asked to explain why. There was a farmer who lived near Casino del Monte who had lost a leg in the First World War and had a wooden one. Naturally it was difficult for him to walk to the church of Mercatale. It was a long way and the track was much rougher than it is now. Then he had to stand during the Mass, which he found very tiring. But Groppa Secca didn't like to see the man skipping Mass, so he said to him, 'You come to Mass and you can sit on my bench, I'll stand up myself.' So the poor peasant was compelled to attend Mass every Sunday.

Groppa Secca's house in Mercatale was called the Villino, and it was the grandest house in the village. It was on a small hill above the other houses, to show that here lived a superior being. He lived there with his sister Maria. She was even nastier than he was, and you can understand why she never got married. She used to give her washing to a peasant's wife – she couldn't do it herself because she was a fine lady. When the peasant brought the clean clothes back she would throw them on the table and inspect them garment by garment. She would say, 'This is all right, this isn't, nor this,' and she would throw those she considered to be still dirty on to the floor. So the peasant had to take some of the clothes back to his wife to get them washed again. But those garments weren't really dirty. She behaved like that on purpose just to give more work to the peasant's wife and to humiliate her.

When I was about ten years old I took some ricotta to Mistress Maria. It was nearly two miles from Casa del Bosco to the Villino and I had to carry the basin carefully to avoid spilling it or getting it dirty. I gave her the ricotta, she took it into the house, and then came out again to give me back the bowl, saying, 'Wait a moment, I have something to give you.' So I sat down on the bench outside the door and tried to guess what she was going to bring me. Certainly not money, as she was as miserly as her brother. A handful of walnuts or almonds, perhaps, or some sweets, or even a roll with a slice of meat in it? I waited and waited with my mouth watering and finally the lady appeared at the window holding something out to me. 'Say a prayer for me,' she said and closed the window. Do you know what she had given me? A broken umbrella handle! I was so disappointed that I felt like crying. On the way home I threw the object into some brambles. It's probably still there.

Groppa Secca was the only person in the village who had a car.

It was a *Balilla* and it was big and black. He didn't drive himself, he had a driver. He only used the car on Thursdays, when he went to the market, so people could see how important he was. Then Mussolini put a tax on unmarried men. One day Groppa Secca said to his driver, 'We are going to Florence.' So the driver took him to Florence. When they arrived Groppa Secca got out of the car and said, 'Now there are two of us, but when I come back there will be three of us.' And after a short time he came back accompanied by a lady. She wasn't dressed as a bride, so he must have married her on another occasion. She can't have been his mistress because such a thing would have been unthinkable in those days. I know that at the Villino they slept in separate bedrooms, because my sister Marsiglia who was working there as a maid said she would have seen if they had slept together. I'm sure he married her to avoid paying that tax, not because he had fallen in love with her. I don't think he was capable of falling in love. He had no more sentiment in him than a dried herring.

Groppa Secca's wife was younger than he was but she died first. It was better to die than to go on living with Groppa Secca, because he got nastier and nastier as he grew older. So he was alone once more. But after the war he began to feel his age and hired a bailiff. The man was called Pietro and he and his wife came to live in the Villino. He started to run the property, though I'm sure Groppa Secca watched his every move. The old man died in 1962 at the age of ninety-seven. He had always eaten the same things, broth, boiled chicken and white wine. Apparently we must eat like that if we want a long life. When he died I went to the funeral, partly because it was the custom but also because I wanted to make sure that he was properly buried and would never come back to torment us.

CHAPTER 3

Fascism and the War

Groppa Secca had not been a Fascist, but it was not his ideological convictions that brought about his reluctance to join the ruling party. The local Fascists needed somewhere to hold their meetings and they compelled Groppa Secca to hand over a room that was part of his property opposite the square in Mercatale. Attached as he was to his possessions, he objected strongly to this expropriation, and this led him to hate those who had carried it out. In fact, not all the landowners were pro-Fascist, for one reason or another. But, like Groppa Secca, they kept their mouths shut because, by virtue of their social status, they approved of a certain aspect of Fascism: its policy of keeping both peasants and workers in a state of submission and therefore of suppressing the trade union movement.

The Fascists like to recruit people into the Party as young as possible. Before children went to school they became '*Figli o Figlie della Lupa*', and once they started school the male children between the ages of eight and ten could become *Balilla*. The teacher told us that this was the nickname of a young Genoese boy who in 1746, enraged by the sight of the Austrians occupying his city, threw a stone at some soldiers, thus setting off a successful uprising against the invaders. She said, 'You must be courageous like that young boy, and even throw a stone if the situation requires it.' A lot of stone-throwing went on in the playground during break . . . but no one said we were heroes. They said, 'You young devils, if you break a window you're in for a beating!' The village boys joined the association but not the peasants' children: they didn't have the money to buy the uniform, and anyway they were shy and didn't want to draw attention to themselves. The *Balilla* wore black shirts with grey-green shorts and long socks, while the girls, the *Piccole Italiane*, wore black skirts with white blouses, but only a few had proper shoes, and those with clogs felt ashamed. When compulsory education was over the boys became *Giovani Fascisti* or Young Fascists. They wore black shirts with black ties and grey-green jackets and long trousers. They also wore military boots and gaiters, which they were very proud of as they marched around. I know someone who became a *Giovane Fascista* solely on account of those boots and gaiters! When they were eighteen they became army cadets. Every Saturday afternoon they went to the Fascist headquarters in Mercatale and studied military theory. They would sing the famous Fascist song '*Giovinezza*':

Giovinezza, giovinezza,	Youth, youth,
Primavera di bellezza,	Springtime of beauty,
Nella gloria e nell'asprezza	In times of glory, in times of hardship
Il tuo canto squilla e va.	Your song continues to resound.
All'arme, all'arme!	To arms, to arms!
All'arme, siamo fascisti,	To arms, we are Fascists,
Terrori dei comunisti,	Terror of the Communists,
E non si son mai visti	They never show their faces
Perché hanno paura	Because they are afraid
Della bastonatura!	Of being beaten up!

Then they shouted 'Long live the Duce', making the Fascist salute. The louder they shouted the more important they felt. The Secretary of the local section would cry, 'Fascists, here's to us, hip, hip . . .,' and they would reply, 'Hurrah!'

When the *Giovani Fascisti* had finished their course they considered themselves proper soldiers. They were given imitation rifles and cartridge pouches and they would march around the streets singing patriotic songs. The Italian army has always taught soldiers to march and sing songs, it's only waging wars they're not so good at. Every now and then they would stop and do some drill with their imitation rifles. On public holidays, or the anniversary of some important date like 28 October 1922 when Mussolini came to power or 4 November 1918 when the First World War ended, all the young people would go to the Fascist headquarters to put on their uniforms and then they would congregate in the square. First they would make a procession: the section leaders would march in front, followed by the *Giovani Fascisti* with their imitation rifles, and then came the *Balilla* and the *Piccole Italiane*, after them the *Figli e Figlie della Lupa*, and last of all came everybody else. The procession would march as far as La Torre and then back again to the square, where some local bigwig would be waiting for them and he would make a speech. He would say that we must be valiant and always ready to face the Enemy, because the Duce said there were Enemies everywhere. Then he said that we must have more children so that there would be more soldiers to fight the Enemy (he didn't really make clear who the Enemy was, however). He then recounted all the wonderful things the regime had accomplished for its citizens and told us what laws had been passed recently. The people stood round and listened. They were rather diffident but they had always heard only one version of the facts. The few newspapers that circulated were in the hands of the Fascists and the radio too was full of propaganda. People didn't know what to believe, so they just stood there in silence. The meeting ended with the usual ritual: the Secretary would shout, 'Long live the Duce!' and then, 'Fascists, here's to us, hip, hip . . .,' and the young people would shout at the top of their lungs, 'Hurrah!' and then they would all disperse.

Being the child of a peasant, I didn't belong to any of these associations but I used to go to the meetings on public holidays because I enjoyed watching everyone marching about. After all, I spent most of my days alone in the woods and it was nice to see a bit of jollity and movement for a change. But when they talked about war and the Enemy my father would look sad and shake his head. In theory he was a Fascist too, as he was a member of the party. But if he hadn't been, the *squadristi* would have been sent to beat him up. This happened to a lot of people, to Tinacci of Rendola, for example: they beat him up and for four years they wouldn't give him a work permit. But he didn't join the party all the same – he was a very courageous fellow! Many people, among them my father, joined out of fear, just so that they would be left in peace to get on with their work and bring up their families. But he certainly didn't believe in the Fascist cause and he hated the idea of war. Both he and his brother Pietro had dug out trenches during the First World War and they knew that wars brought only suffering and death.

The local party secretary was a landowner. He had only two farms, yet this enabled him to lead an easy life. He was rather a comic fellow, when he wore his uniform he strutted around looking like a village Mussolini. Now and then some bigwig would come to Mercatale and he would put on his belted jacket with plus fours and black boots and a military cap like the ones soldiers wear, and he would stick out his chest like a cock bantam. But he was rather stupid and everybody laughed at him behind his back.

During the meetings in the square of Mercatale our leaders began to promise us 'a place in the sun'. I would have thought that the Italians had plenty of places in the sun in their own country, not to speak of Eritrea, Libya and Somalia, our colonies, but our leaders considered that we needed to go to Abyssinia to find some more. After all, countries like England and France had big empires, so Italy had the right to have one too. But that was all we knew about the matter, because there weren't any newspapers in Mercatale then, just *L'Avvenire d'Italia*, the one which was delivered to Groppa Secca. It was published by the Vatican and he used to read it rather furtively, as he didn't want any of his workers to read it too. Evidently he wanted to be the only person in the village who knew what was happening in Italy.

Then one day in 1935, I think it was, all the church bells round about began to ring: Italy had declared war on Abyssinia, because its inhabitants were uncivilized and it was our duty to bring civilization to them (whether they liked it or not). And by so doing we could acquire that place in the sun we needed so much. Consequently many of those who had done military service were called up. In all households people were terrified that the fatal postcard calling the menfolk to arms would arrive at any time. In fact one of my brothers-in-law received such a postcard and was sent off to Eritrea, where they were planning the attack on Abyssinia. Later on he told us that the black people there were as poor and wretched as ourselves, and you could hardly have called it a war because when our soldiers invaded Abyssinia they were not met by a proper army, just a terrified population who ran out of their huts and took flight as our army approached. Only the women were left behind and they were an easy prey for our valiant conquerors.

In fact it was at that time we began to hear the song '*Faccetta nera*'. It began like this:

Faccetta nera, bell'abissina,	Little black face, pretty Abyssinian maid,
Aspetta e spera, che già l'ora s'avvicina,	Wait and hope, as the time is drawing near,
Quando saremo a Mogalè	When we get to Mogalè
Noi ti daremo un'altra Legge e un altro Re!	We'll give you a new Law and a new King!

But those who were against the war used to change the last line in this way:

Noi piglieremo, noi piglieremo quello che c'è!	We'll grab, we'll grab everything there is!

Some Fascists went as volunteers to Abyssinia. They must have thought that fighting wars was all marching and singing. A fellow from Montevarchi went and when he came back he told us this story. One day he entered a village and an African greeted him, saying, 'Salaam!' And our bold soldier replied, 'You call me a salami? Nobody has ever dared to call me that!' and he knocked the man down. When we heard the story we all laughed, but now I know that the poor African was only being polite and he didn't deserve to be treated in that way.

So now Italy had a big empire like other countries, but for us peasants life went on as before: whether there was a war or whether there wasn't we still had to dig and plough and sow. Perhaps this was our salvation, because instead of worrying about winning wars, we worried about whether the rain would ruin our hay or whether there was enough grain for our bread, and so life went on from day to day.

Apparently, however, Mussolini still didn't consider our empire big enough and when he saw his friend Hitler invading Europe he didn't want to seem inferior so he invaded Albania. Italy would then have even more room for its inhabitants and it was best to conquer as much land as possible while the going was good, seeing that the Duce had eight million bayonets and they had to be put to use somehow.

In a few months Hitler had occupied half of Europe. He obviously had the winning team so on 10 June Mussolini declared war on the Enemy too – yes, he had finally found one. I remember that day because everyone had come to the square to listen to Mussolini on the radio. I went along too, more because I was curious to hear a voice coming all the way from Rome than for the content of his speech. I was only just thirteen and I didn't really know what going to war meant. After all, the war in Abyssinia hadn't affected our lives very much. I don't remember much about what he said, just the slogans that were also written on walls all over the place, like: 'Italians, the Fateful Hour has come, by the Will of the Italian

People, of the Duce and of God. We must Win and Win we shall!' Notice how God came after the Duce.

One of the older peasants asked how could the Duce be so sure that we would win, but he said it under his breath and nobody had time to reply because on the radio there was a roar of applause in Piazza Venezia where Mussolini was haranguing the crowd. So the people of Mercatale applauded too and that way felt they were doing their duty as good Italians. I didn't clap myself, not because I thought the whole idea was absurd, but because I was too shy.

After the meeting I went home and told my family what I had heard. They all grew sad and my mother said, 'So now there's going to be another war! If our menfolk are called to arms who's going to work the land?' I reassured her, saying that the war would be over soon, that it would only last two or three months (that's what they said on the radio). 'They may not even need our menfolk, mother.' But my brother said, 'What fools they are, it's like hitting your head against a brick wall! They said the last war would be short and it lasted three years. I expect it'll be the same story this time.' But he said it quietly as he was afraid someone might hear him. The regime had put posters all over the place depicting the Enemy with his ear pressed to the wall, and underneath was written: 'Keep your lips sealed, the Enemy is listening to you!' So we began to think Churchill or Stalin or Roosevelt were lying in wait behind an olive tree, or even in the house, hidden in a cupboard or behind a wine barrel.

At the beginning of the war there were only six of us in the house: my mother, two of my sisters, my cousin Edoardo, my brother Azeglio and me. Soon afterwards Gigi came to be our *garzone*. He came from a large family, so his parents sent him and his brother to work in other families. They were not paid but at least they had enough to eat. Gigi was more or less my age and he began to take over my work, looking after the pigs and the sheep in the woods. So I was free to do other jobs. And thank goodness

Azeglio, Pietro's brother, serving as a groom in the Italian army.

for that, because soon the two men in the family were called to arms. First Edoardo was sent to Libya to join the infantry. Later he fell ill with malaria and was sent home to convalesce. As soon as he was better they sent him off to Greece. Obviously the war couldn't manage without him. Azeglio was luckier because he didn't have to fight, he looked after the army horses, first in Pisa then in Yugoslavia. The officers always went round on horseback, so that they could be distinguished from the common soldiers, while other horses, and mules too, were used to pull the cannons.

So at thirteen I had to do a man's work. I ploughed the land with the oxen, I pruned and dug, I sowed and mowed, all the jobs that a farmer had to do and that my cousin Edoardo had taught me. Luckily I was strong and healthy and was not afraid of hard work. You see such skimpy-looking boys about nowadays, with arms as thin as spaghetti. If they had to work like I did they would collapse after a day or two. Naturally my mother and sisters helped me. Then when we needed a bit of extra help, like at harvest-time, we called Gino dei Cini, the boy who hid in the oil jar. My mother paid him out of the subsidy, the money the government gave to farming families when their menfolk had gone to war. But we did most of the work ourselves. We were used to working from dawn till dusk and didn't think anything of it.

In spite of all that hard labour I still found time one way or another to hear how the war was progressing. For example, Brucio, a bicycle mechanic at the bottom of the square of Mercatale, had gone to Abyssinia as a volunteer and then he had worked in a quarry, so he had saved up some money. He bought this little shop and managed to make a living. As he had been to Africa he was able to find it on a map. In fact, he had a map of the world pinned up in his workshop and every time someone asked him where our troops had got to he showed us the place with the tip of his finger. But his hands were always covered with grease and when it happened that the troops neither advanced nor retreated (I think it was near Alexandria in Egypt), the place on the map got so greasy that you couldn't make it out any more. It must have been El Alamein, where later there was a great battle and our army was defeated. It was a stroke of luck for our poor soldiers, at least for those who survived, because many of them were taken prisoner. It was better to be a prisoner-of-war than to fight in a war they didn't see the point of. If Italians have to defend their own country, then they fight like lions! But they couldn't have cared less about Africa.

During the war a *sfollato*, an evacuee, came to live at Le Muricce. He had an electrical shop in Montevarchi (his son still has it), and he also used to sell radios. We couldn't use a radio because we had no electricity, so this kind man solved the problem by bringing us a crystal set. We didn't understand how it worked, but when you put on a pair of headphones you could listen to the news about the war. We heard about the victories of our troops in Africa, about how they had conquered many villages without meeting resistance from the Enemy, and then we heard about all the gallant actions of our soldiers. At the end of the bulletin they gave the last bit of news which was always the same: 'One of our aircraft did not return to base.' After a few months I began to think, if every day one of our aircraft doesn't return to base, how many planes and how many pilots have we lost? The authorities didn't count them up, but I did.

The most reliable source of news was Radio Londra. A fellow who lived beside the river Tricesimo in Mercatale had a powerful radio and we spent some evenings listening to that. It usually gave us a quite different version of the facts. The Fascist authorities didn't want us to hear about the Italian defeats, only about the victories, so before turning on the radio we would bolt the door and close all the shutters.

We would also hear scraps of news from soldiers coming home on leave, and they too told us what had really happened. I remember, for example, what we were told by Giotto, a farmer from Mercatale. The Italian army in Africa were using the same cannons that my father had used on Mont Blanc during the First World War. They had wooden wheels that worked very well in the mountains because of the cold. But in the desert where it was forty degrees centigrade in the shade (just imagine then how hot it was in the sun!) those wooden wheels began to split.

Those who came back from Russia had the worst stories to tell. Many never came back at all. Hitler was out of his mind to think of invading Russia, hadn't he read the history books? Not even Napoleon managed to conquer it. It is too vast and the winter is long and terrible. They say it was an even more powerful Enemy than the Russians. I read later that Hitler didn't want the Italians to go to war in Russia, only the Germans. After the war in Africa he probably realized that the Italian army wasn't as well equipped as his, and maybe the soldiers did not fight as well. They certainly had less motivation. But Mussolini was determined to send along an Italian army, because he was afraid that Hitler would have Russia all to himself. We heard a lot of propaganda on the wireless about this new front, and many volunteers went joyfully off to fight. I remember two young fellows from Montevarchi who had signed up. They were only nineteen or twenty years of age. The evening before their departure they came to our house to say goodbye. 'We'll only be away a couple of months, three at most,' they said, 'and when we come back we will be given any job we want!' But they never came back. Like so many others they were reported missing: if they hadn't fallen in battle they must have died of cold and hunger, either on the march back or in a Russian concentration camp. Poor boys, they couldn't even have found Russia on the map. A fellow called Scatizzi from Cavriglia understood the situation better. When he heard the Fascists rejoicing about the advance in Russia he said under his breath:

*State attenti, perché quello che
   conquistate metro per metro*
Dopo di corsa lo farete indietro.
	Be careful, because what you conquer
	   yard by yard
	Later you will have to cover again at
	   a run.

And that is exactly what happened.

A fellow called Nando did make it back after the Armistice, and he's still alive to tell the tale. During the retreat the soldiers passed through an area where there were still stooks of wheat under the snow. He and his fellow soldiers stripped off the ears of corn and with a little handmill that he had made they ground them into flour. Then they heated some water and put the flour into it. That was how they managed to survive. Another was Orazio, the gamewarden of the Rendola estate. He went to Russia as a postman because he could read and write better than the others and could make out the addresses on the envelopes. He came back to Mercatale on leave, but he realized that his return to Russia would have been a death sentence, so he went behind a barn and shot off a couple of fingers. He was sent to hospital and remained in Italy. Of course he said that it was an accident, but nobody believed him. How could you blame him? If he had gone back to Russia he would have died.

The two menfolk of our family were luckier. They had a terrible time but at least they came back from the war unscathed. A letter arrived punctually every month from my cousin Edoardo in Greece and my brother in Yugoslavia. They always contained the same news, that they were well and hoped to come home soon. The letters were written by a friend because they couldn't read or write themselves.

Towards the end of the year 1942 people began to talk about exemptions from military service for those who had families to maintain. At Castelnuovo dei Sabbioni there were mines where lignite, a kind of coal, was extracted. If a peasant came home to work in the mine he could live at home and work on the land in his free time. But only the *padrone* could apply for an exemption, not the family. We discussed this possibility at home and in the end it was decided that I should speak to Groppa Secca about it. I was fifteen at the time and still very shy, but I so longed to have Edoardo home again that I plucked up the necessary courage. One

Sunday evening I walked down to the farm storehouses opposite the square of Mercatale. Groppa Secca had just locked up and had started to walk towards the Villino. As soon as he noticed me I greeted him, saying, 'Good evening, *padrone*.' He was rather surprised to see me and asked what I wanted at that hour. I didn't reply but began to follow him as he walked slowly home. I walked a few steps behind him because I was only a peasant and it wouldn't have been considered correct to have walked beside him. At last he addressed me again and I told him that I had come to ask him to apply for an exemption for my cousin Edoardo. But he looked grim and didn't reply until we had reached the Villino: he clearly didn't feel he could put me out of my misery by granting my request immediately. Finally he turned to me and said, 'All right, I'll apply for the exemption, but if everybody comes home who is going to carry on waging the war?' As if the war concerned him more than the farmwork. 'At your service, *padrone*,' I said. 'You may go,' he answered. 'May you have a pleasant evening, *padrone*,' I said in reply. It was customary to address the *padrone* with these words, as if he were the Lord Almighty.

As soon as the famous exemption arrived we sent it off to my cousin in Greece, hoping that he hadn't been killed in the meantime. But some weeks later he came back and took up work at the mine. It was ten miles away and he had to cover the distance by bicycle twice every working day. He would leave very early because his shift was from six o'clock in the morning to two in the afternoon. He was therefore able to spend some hours in the fields and the farm began to be well looked after again. I remember that at that time I had to plough the fields after the harvest. It was summertime and very hot, so Edoardo and I would get up when it was still dark, at about four o'clock. He would help me to harness the oxen to the plough, then I would go into the fields and he would bicycle off to work. He had a long day, but at least he didn't have to risk dying in battle. I used to plough until nine o'clock, and then I would put the oxen back in the stable and give

Ploughing with oxen.

them food and water. At this point I was ravenous, so I would go to the vegetable garden and pick a couple of tomatoes and an onion and eat them with bread and a little oil. We always ate the same things, but we couldn't complain. In those days it was a luxury to have enough to eat at all.

When Italy conquered Abyssinia the rest of the world expressed their disapproval by imposing sanctions. So the Fascist regime had to introduce rationing, and this continued when the Second World War broke out. Rationing was applied to salt, sugar, bread, rice, coffee and tobacco. I think cloth, too, and maybe other things, but they didn't really concern us because we wouldn't have been able to afford them anyway. The *Comune* gave us a ration book and we had to tear off coupons in it when we bought something. But it was worse for people living in towns, we weren't so badly off. We had our own vegetables, chickens, wine, oil, sheep's cheese and so on. As for the things that were rationed, we could use our own honey instead of sugar, we made our own pasta, we made coffee with toasted acorns, and made food more tasty with herbs that we grew in the garden or found in the fields. But we did have to buy matches and salt. When we bought matches we were very careful not to waste them, and as for salt, we could find it on the black market. It was brought to us by a fellow whose nickname was Ventena, the name of the village he came from. He would set off from the Arno valley on his bicycle and go all the way to the saltworks of Volterra near the coast, a good fifty miles away and all on untarmacked roads. The saltworks were run by the government, but the local peasants used to gather salt on the sly and sell it on the black market. It was coarse and full of earth, but that always went to the bottom of the pot. We were used to eating earth anyway, as our vegetables came from the garden and we didn't have enough water to wash them properly. When Ventena came back with his sack of salt he would sell a kilo or two to each of the local housewives and in return they would give him some beans or a bottle of olive oil.

The greatest problem was bread. We didn't buy it with the ration book because we had our own grain, but even that was rationed. At harvest-time an official came up from the town hall of Montevarchi to supervise the weighing of the sacks, and of course Groppa Secca and the fieldwarden were present too. We could keep two quintals of grain for every member of the family. That was two hundred kilos and it seems a lot, but it amounted to only three or four slices of bread per person a day. In those days we ate bread for breakfast, bread for lunch and bread for supper, so the ration wasn't nearly enough to satisfy our hunger. The official was understanding about this, because at a certain point he would say, 'Well, folks, I'm going to go into the woods for a little nap, you carry on.' He wanted to give us the chance to steal a bit of grain, but it was impossible with Groppa Secca there – he was too afraid of being found out.

Now and then we managed to find some grain on the black market. I remember once taking the ox cart from Mercatale up to Nusenna at the dead of night. The oxen plodded along very slowly, and it took a long time. A relation of ours had managed to procure for us two quintals of grain. I paid twenty-six thousand lire for it, an enormous sum in those days: it was all the money that Edoardo had earned at the mine, plus the subsidy that my mother had received because my brother was in Yugoslavia. We were left penniless, but at least we had enough grain to last until the following harvest. I had hidden a thick stick in the ox cart to use in case I was attacked by thieves. I was only fifteen years old but I was ready for anything. If I didn't take that grain home my family would starve. Luckily I met no one.

Then there was the problem of getting the grain ground into flour. Even the mill was controlled by the authorities, so we had to get the job done at night. After supper I would put a sack on my back and go cross-country to the mill, avoiding the main tracks. The miller was ready for us, but he always pretended to be afraid to grind our grain because it was illegal to do so. He would say, 'If they catch us I'll be ruined!' So he made me stand outside to keep a lookout. Nobody ever came, but in the meantime he was able to pinch a bit of our grain. Then with this he was able to bribe the inspectors, though he probably kept a bit back for himself. One can hardly blame him. He had to make a living like anybody else.

But even with that grain bought on the black market we didn't have enough. So when we made the bread we would add some maize or potato flour. As a result the bread was not nearly so good. We made the bread every Saturday, so that it would be fresh on Sunday. But after about two days it became hard and rough, it was like eating a cheese grater. If you put it into your mouth too quickly it would cut your palate. But we had to eat it as it was all we had, and how would we have energy to work otherwise? I remember once we were sitting at the table and my mother said, 'Appetite makes the best food.' She was right, because when you are fifteen years old you would eat anything, even lumps of old iron. Though we didn't even have any iron – we had had to hand it in because of the war. When we listened to the war bulletins on the crystal set and we heard that our side had bombed London, or some other town belonging to the Enemy, we imagined that the bombs had been made out of our old tools and ploughshares, and this troubled us.

Talking about ploughshares, I'll tell you what happened in the spring of 1943. I was in the house and my brother ran in looking distraught. 'Come quickly, the bees are swarming, listen to them buzzing, go and get the ploughshare!' You may not know that when the queen bee flies up she makes a special kind of hum that induces all the other bees to follow her, and often they all fly away to make a nest elsewhere. But if we make a loud noise they can't hear her any more and they stop following her. She then goes down to a tree and, as they are confused, they follow her and form a mass. That's when we can catch them and put them into a hive. So I went to the plough and removed the ploughshare and also the screw that fixes it to the plough and began to knock them together. I knocked with all my might but the humming noise went on, in fact it got louder and louder. 'What the devil,' I said, 'where are those damn bees?' Then I heard some loud bangs and saw some bombers flying in formation along the bottom of the valley. They were spewing out bombs – you could see them falling because they glistened in the sun. They were Allied planes and they had come to bomb the railway bridges, one near Bucine and the other beyond Caposelvi. Not bees at all, quite a different story! That was the first time the bombers appeared. Later on they came quite often so we got used to the noise.

This episode reminds me of Corrido, a Fascist who lived in Mercatale. Every morning he walked four miles to guard the railway bridge at Bucine. If a formation passed he would shoot at it. I can't imagine what he thought he was doing. It was like throwing a pebble at a herd of elephants. When he came back people at the *bottega* asked him, 'But aren't you afraid?' 'Afraid, me?' he would say. 'Look, this is Corrido,' and he would point at himself. 'This is another Corrido,' and he would point at his gun. 'And here's another Corrido, and another, and another,' he said showing everybody his cartridge pouch. 'There are ten of us or more, how can we be afraid?' And the shopkeeper would pour him another glass of wine because he was a Fascist too.

CHAPTER 4

After the Armistice

By 1943 we began to realize that, in spite of all the optimistic propaganda on the Italian radio, we might lose the war. As a result of the campaign in Africa, Italy had lost all her colonies, including the ones she had before the war began. We had no more place in the sun! It was clear to everybody that the invasion of Russia had been a disaster, with thousands of Italian solders killed or missing on the steppes. Then we heard the dramatic news that affected us more closely: the Allies had landed in Sicily. At this point Mussolini was totally discredited, so we were not surprised to hear on Radio Londra that he had been forced to resign by those who had been his closest cronies. The King appointed General Badoglio to come out of retirement and lead the government and Mussolini was imprisoned in a hotel in the Abruzzi mountains east of Rome.

By this time we were listening to Radio Londra every day, as the situation was constantly changing. Apparently Badoglio had been negotiating secretly with the Allies, and on 8 September, a date carved in the memory of all Italians who lived through the war, he signed the Armistice, just as the Allies were crossing over to the mainland. As a result German troops flooded the country like a swarm of angry bees. Instead of staying in the capital and facing the danger like everybody else, Badoglio and the King ran away to Brindisi, on the Adriatic coast. I think the Italians never forgave the monarchy for this act of cowardice. At this point the

Germans rescued Mussolini and put him at the head of a new government, the Republic of Salò, in the north of Italy. But he no longer counted for much, it was the Germans who were in command. The Allies continued to fight their way up the south of Italy and when the Badoglio goverment saw how the land lay they declared war on Germany. Our former allies had become the Enemy!

There hadn't been many Germans around until the Armistice. They had an observation point at Monteluco, the mountain above Nusenna. Five or six of them were stationed there, and they would go about in a truck. I saw them now and then when they stopped for a beer at the *bottega* at Mercatale. They did us no harm, but those who fought in the First World War hated them all the same. But power was still in the hands of the local Fascists, like our party secretary in Mercatale, and not surprisingly the Germans entrusted everything to them. They were all Fascists together. But after the Armistice the Germans were everywhere. Gradually the Allies advanced up the country, but the Germans did everything they could to push them back. We used to listen to Radio Londra and every day there was a new instalment. It was like a soap opera on the television, but more serious because people were getting killed. I remember when the Allies took Naples and were then stopped by the German front at Cassino. Finally they broke through, but the fighting was fierce and in the battle the famous monastery there was razed to the ground. The Allies continued to advance and finally they captured Rome.

From 8 September onwards much of the Italian army was disbanded. My brother Azeglio in Yugoslavia had a stroke of luck: he was in Fiume at the time and saw a ship in the port. 'Where's this ship going?' 'To Italy.' 'I'm coming too!' And he got on at once. He didn't even have his rucksack with him. So he was with us again that autumn. Other soldiers weren't so lucky: many were sent to work camps in Germany and died there of hunger and disease.

For the soldiers who were in Italy there was a period of great confusion and often orders were followed by counter-orders, so they didn't know what to do. Italy was no longer on Germany's side, and in the end only those that were convinced Fascists remained faithful to the cause. Most of the others laid down their arms and made for home. In our valley there was a constant coming and going, as soldiers who came from the south but found themselves in the north went towards home, while those who came from the north but found themselves in the south went home in the opposite direction. But these soldiers didn't go along the bottom of the valley because there were too many Germans down there. They followed the electric pylons halfway up the Chianti hills. When darkness fell they would stop and ask the farmers for help. Our house was not far from the line of pylons, so we often gave these fugitives a bed and something to eat. Sometimes we would give them some old clothes to wear, so that they would no longer look like soldiers. The Germans considered them to be traitors and if they found them they would send them to those work camps in Germany, where they would probably have died of hardship like so many others.

The Italian Fascists too, at least the more fanatical ones, sought out the deserters. They would go into the houses to look for young men born in 1924 or 1925, and would send them to do military service or to work for TODT, the German engineers whose work was to repair the railways and bridges that the Allies had bombed. Many lads hid in the country, but at Easter they returned home to visit their families and the Fascists surprised them there, the villains. Brunero, the fellow who had been breastfed as a baby by my mother, stayed with us when he was hiding from the Fascists. He was safe with us because nobody else knew he had come from Nusenna. He used to work in the fields with us during the day and when it was dark his father would bring him some food because he knew that we had little to spare.

Brunero had a friend called Fernando who had hidden himself

up at Sinciano, the village in the hills above us where his grandfather lived. Fernando was ingenious and made a trumpet out of chestnut bark. When he blew it it made a bellowing noise so loud that we could hear it from Casa del Bosco. Then Brunero made a similar trumpet and they agreed that if the Germans approached they would warn each other with a blast on the trumpet.

Some of these lads became partisans. They didn't hide in our hills, where it would have been easy to find them, but on Pratomagno, the mountain on the other side of the valley. It is nearly five thousand feet high and is thickly wooded. They would sleep in abandoned farmhouses and the local farmers would give them something to eat. They would be joined by ex-soldiers, and others who were wanted by the Fascists for one reason or another. There were also a few criminals among them. There was one, for example, who was reputed to have killed two or three people. After the war the Communists put a photograph of him up in the *Casa del Popolo*, their local headquarters. Later on they took it down – I expect they too had heard about the murders.

After the Armistice the Arno valley was in turmoil. When Mussolini fell the anti-Fascists sent off the *Podestà* and other Fascists (they even beat up some of them) and they chose a new mayor, a local lawyer called Mr Borsari. But when Mussolini was freed by the Germans and became head of the government at Salò, the Fascists reappeared and they tore off Mr Borsari's moustaches. He died soon after, perhaps as a result of this brutal act.

It was at this time that the partisans killed the Fascist party secretary of Loro Ciuffenna, a village at the foot of Pratomagno. The Fascists buried him in the cemetery of Montevarchi. After the ceremony there were the usual Fascist slogans and then Maratti and Pasqualino, two of the most fanatical Fascists, declared with their hands on their chests: 'Baroni, we will follow you!' And two years later that's what they did, because they were killed by the crowd in Via Isidoro, the street where the carters kept their horses.

In 1943 the Fascists naturally supported the Salò Republic; but they felt less sure of themselves. On the other hand the anti-Fascists got bolder and bolder as the Allies advanced. In the square opposite the post office of Montevarchi there was a statue of Giuseppe Garibaldi, our great national hero, and one night somebody wrote on the pedestal: '*Scendi Beppe ci risono!*' 'Come down, Beppe, they're back again!'

In the spring of 1944 there was a lot of troop movement in the Arno valley as the Germans prepared to resist the Allied advance. The retreat began in June and continued all through the month of July. But a month before, the Germans had stationed a Gestapo command at the *fattoria* of Rendola. The officers lived in the owners' villa, while the ordinary soldiers were billeted in the farmhouses. No social mixing there! At Le Muricce, which was only two hundred yards away from our house, some German officers took up residence in the house while the owner was still living there, with the soldiers billeted in the farmhouse next door. One day one of the soldiers stole a duck from the peasant, who immediately reported the theft to the commanding officer. The offender was summoned, the officer made him stand against a wall and made as if to shoot him. He didn't actually do it, but he made the soldier understand that he had behaved incorrectly. The German officers were very punctilious and severe with their own soldiers, not only with us Italians.

Often the Germans came to the farmers' houses to order them to do some job or other. Once we had to dig out some level pieces of ground for cannons, though in the end they didn't bring the cannons there. I suppose it was too late. Five or six of us were digging away while three young soldiers sat under a tree playing cards. Their rifles were propped up against the tree and we could easily have overpowered them. We could even have killed them, but we were too frightened to do so and, after all, they hadn't done us any harm.

But others had every reason to resent the Germans because sometimes they carried women away to rape them. One of these women was married and had children. Luckily none of them got pregnant. Then the women learnt a trick. A plant called *l'erba dell'amore*, the love plant, grew in the fields. It has fat, juicy leaves and if the women squashed them and rubbed the juice over their legs and arms, the next day they would be covered with a nasty rash. It looked as if they had some skin disease, so the German soldiers would leave them alone. They didn't touch any girl that looked dirty, either. They liked women who looked clean as well as pretty. As you can imagine, after a few unpleasant episodes no more suitable women were to be found: they either rubbed themselves with that juice or stopped washing themselves. These were the only ways to avoid being raped.

The Germans who were stationed in our countryside, at Rendola and Le Muricce, had to eat like anybody else and naturally they expected the peasants to supply them with food and drink now that they were enemies. German soldiers often went round looking for eggs, chickens and so on. About a month before the retreat it was rumoured at Rendola that the soldiers were going to take away all our oxen. Now, for a peasant it was a disaster to lose his oxen because he used them for ploughing, pulling carts and all the other jobs on the farm. So that night the peasants took their oxen up to Vie Piane, about a mile and a half above the village. But in the evening it had rained, so when the German soldiers came to take the oxen they saw the hoofprints in the mud. Naturally they followed these and found the hidden oxen. They sent the poor creatures down to the *fattoria* of Rendola and later they were taken away to be slaughtered. We were more fortunate with our oxen, though we had taken them to the woods too. Chimintelli, the carter, came along with a couple of horses, and Gostino, who used to drive a cart round to buy animal hides, brought a horse too. We also took our pigs with all their piglets. As soon as we got up to the woods we hurriedly made some enclosures out of branches and put the animals in them to stop them wandering home. The place wasn't far from Vie Piane, but we went up before it began to rain, so we left no tracks. When the German soldiers drove the other oxen down the animals bellowed in distress and ours wanted to bellow back, but we held their mouths shut and they weren't discovered.

We couldn't keep our animals up in the woods for long because there was no food for them, so we took them to our neighbours at Casino del Monte, the house where I was born. The Germans had already taken their oxen away so it was unlikely that they would return. Peasants used to help each other in this way, otherwise who else would help you? When we got home we cleaned out our stables so that it was clear we had no oxen left, and moved all the hay and straw away from in front of the house.

However, the Germans still came to our house to look for food. You couldn't refuse to give them anything, otherwise they would make you pay dearly. They took our pigs and our sheep, our turkeys and our ducks. Everything except the hens, but of course they wanted the eggs, and we had to hide those if we wanted to eat them ourselves. The soldiers stationed at Rendola took away one of our calves. They slaughtered it and sent us back the head – I don't know whether out of kindness or out of spite.

One day some German soldiers came to our house, took one of our pigs and shot it then and there. They made me load it on to a wheelbarrow and push it down to a farmhouse beyond Le Muricce. We had almost got there when some Allied fighter-planes appeared in the sky above us. Nearby there was a German anti-aircraft battery. The guns began to fire on the planes and the fighters attacked them. The soldiers grabbed hold of me and dragged me down with them into a ditch. When the fighters had gone I continued to push the wheelbarrow towards our destination. At the farmhouse they took the pig, hung it up in a tree and cut off half of it to eat. The other half was left hanging there. After three days it began to stink, and they must have had to throw it away. This seemed a terrible waste to us, as we never had much meat to eat.

One day I went to visit one of my sisters at the *Crocifisso*, a crossroads on the way to Mercatale, and I saw some Germans. One of them had a swollen leg and he sent me to get some water in a bucket so that he could bathe it. I filled up the bucket with water from a pond, but the water was full of insects so he sent me to get water from the nearest fountain. Then the Germans invited me into the house where they were billeted. They had taken a pig too and were frying bits of it in a pan. They cooked some potatoes in the dripping, but they were all red from the pig's blood and when they offered me some I refused: all that grease looked disgusting to me, as I was used to food cooked in olive oil. When I went out I saw several accordions hanging on the garden fence, I expect they had taken them from a shop. I had always longed to have an accordion and I wanted to steal one, but it was too bulky: I wouldn't have been able to hide it on my person if I had met someone on the way home. If I had asked the soldiers to give me one they might have done so. After all, they had been kind to me, but I lacked the courage. That is why to this day I can only play the mouth organ.

During the retreat a German came to our house and asked us for a calf. Edoardo said to him, 'But can't you see we haven't any calves? Look outside the house. We haven't even got a haystack, how could we feed them?' But the soldier wasn't convinced. He walked out of the kitchen towards the stable. I was in the room where we kept the chaff-cutting machine and on the wall hung all sorts of tools, spades, hoes, axes and so on. When I heard him insisting that we should give him a calf I had an idea: suppose I took one of the axes and hit him on the head? Then I could throw him into the manure pit and nobody would be any the wiser. I actually took down one of the axes, but my brother Azeglio came in at that very moment and grabbed it from me, saying, 'You fool, if you do that they will kill us all!'

Finally, the soldier went away empty-handed, not knowing he had risked losing his life. But my brother was right. At that time the Germans were afraid of the Italians, as we were on the Enemy's side and we outnumbered them, even though they were armed and we were not. They had received orders that if they found one dead German they had to kill ten Italians, whether they were guilty or not. Wars are like that, justice flies out of the window. When the Allies bombed the railway bridge near Caposelvi the Germans found one of their soldiers lying dead nearby. Who knows, he may have been killed by a splinter from one of the bombs. But the Germans were convinced that he had been killed by the partisans, or, as they called them, the rebels. They seized a couple of unfortunate fellows and asked them, 'Where are the rebels who killed this soldier?' The two replied, just to get out of a difficult situation, 'They are far away from here, they are at Borro del Ristolli.' This was a farmhouse in the mountains above Mercatale, but they knew that nobody lived there. The Germans forced the two men to show them the way, but when they arrived and saw that the place was empty they were furious and shot the two Italians dead on the spot. Then they went to Poggio del Fattore, a farmhouse nearby. The house was full of *sfollati*, mostly women, children and old people, but there were some young deserters too. They had come up from the valley because they felt safer near the woods. The Germans said, 'Here are the rebels!' Then they lined them up in front of the house and shot them. Only a thirteen-year-old boy, Giulio, survived the massacre. He was wounded in the hand but he had the presence of mind to throw himself down on the ground with the others. When they had finished shooting the Germans walked along the line of bodies to check that everybody was dead and the boy pretended to be dead too. He lay there for hours among the dead bodies of his family, too frightened to move. At dusk he got up and ran along the ridge to Galatrona where he knew he could find a doctor. A German command was at the villa, so the Italians sent him down to Mercatale. There he found the Red Cross, whose duty it was to look after wounded German soldiers. They asked the boy how he had come to be wounded in the hand and he replied that he had been fired on by an enemy plane while he was walking in the woods. So they bandaged his hand and sent him away.

It was only after the retreat that we heard of all the atrocities committed by the Germans. At Castelnuovo dei Sabbioni, a village above the mines where my cousin Edoardo worked, the Germans drove a number of people into a church and shot them. A Fascist in the village had made a list of all the people the Germans ought to shoot: they must have been anti-Fascists, or simply people the man didn't like. But the Germans weren't interested in names, they just wanted to kill a given number of Italians, so they rounded up all the people they could lay hands on and killed them, including the Fascist who had made the list. I'm sorry about all the others, but I'm glad that the villain got his just deserts.

The Germans killed people in the church at Civitella too. They had gone to Mass there, and the priest was killed as well. I don't know why, perhaps they thought they were 'rebels', perhaps they had found another dead German and wanted to carry out a reprisal. Similar atrocities occurred at Loro Ciuffenna, Palazzuolo and San Giustino: for one dead German they would kill forty or so Italians, mostly women and children. What did they think, that they had killed a German? But sometimes the Germans died without being killed by Italians. At the *Crocifisso*, for example, a German was killed by a mortar. His fellow soldiers buried him there, but evidently they didn't dig the grave deep enough because you could still see the toes of his boots. We saw them for weeks but none of us dared to go near. Once Gostinelli, a friend of mine, went to Monteluco to look for mushrooms and he saw two boots sticking out of the undergrowth. He was barefoot at the time so he was filled with joy and went to retrieve his prize. But a German had been killed and had fallen headfirst into the brambles. His legs were sticking up in the air like a couple of toothpicks. My friend almost fainted from the stench, and then he ran all the way home.

During the weeks of the retreat our house was full of *sfollati*: at one time there were about sixty people sleeping there. They slept everywhere, in the stable, in the room where we kept the chaff-cutter, in the cellar. They didn't have any mattresses, they just slept on straw. Most of them procured their own food, as we had very little left. The Germans had taken away almost everything. Then Nando turned up – it was Nando who had been to Russia and survived during the retreat by digging up the stooks of wheat under the snow and grinding the grain with a handmill. That summer there had been a good harvest and we had plenty of stooks of wheat out in the fields. But the harvesters weren't in operation then, and it would have been dangerous to take the wheat all the way down to the mill. If the Germans found you with a sack of grain on your back they would certainly have taken it from you and they might have shot you into the bargain. Luckily Nando was a genius, and he solved the problem by making another handmill out of two pieces of oakwood. Then we took the grain to one of the rooms, flailed it and sieved it, and then we ground it into flour with the handmill. So there was bread for everybody. What with the flour and what was left of our wine and oil, together with what we had growing in the vegetable garden, we managed to survive.

I remember that on Radio Londra they told us that if we wanted to hide something we should bury it in the ground. In fact we had made a hole out in the fields and in it we had put a chest full of clothes and linen and some flasks of oil. We didn't have anything more valuable than that. Other people had real valuables, and they put them in rooms in their houses and walled them up. But it is always possible to see when plaster is freshly made and the Germans weren't fools. They used to unblock the rooms and carry away everything that had been hidden inside. A certain Lombardi of Mercatale had a fur factory in Montevarchi and had made quite a lot of money out of that, and also, like so many others, out of the black market. He hid all he had in a room and blocked it up, but the Germans discovered it and took everything away. His wife had brought a couple of suitcases up to our house and hidden them in the cupboard under the stairs. Then one day two men arrived dressed as German soldiers (but I think they were Italians). They had taken a horse and cart from the *fattoria* of Petrolo, but they didn't have a proper harness so they used telephone wires. These were to be found lying around everywhere and had come from the field telephones of the German army. The two men came into our house and began to poke around in the stable. A poor fellow who was hiding there came flying out, and he was so white with fear I thought he was going to give up the ghost. But those two men paid no attention to people. They went on searching the house until they found the two suitcases. They opened them, then shut them up again, put them on the cart and drove away. Lombardi's wife got very agitated and ran after them but it was to no avail. Now, how did they know that the suitcases were there? Somebody must have let the cat out of the bag. There were many rascals around at that time who took advantage of the general confusion and stole what they could.

One of the *sfollati* in our house was the cashier of the Banco di Roma. One night a couple of men appeared in German uniforms like the other two. They went round the rooms with a torch, and it was clear that they were looking for somebody. Then they found the cashier and his wife in the cellar and forced them to hand over what money they had. It wasn't very much, about six thousand lire, and the men demanded more, but the wife began to weep, saying that it was all they had. The men said, 'You've already talked too much, come to the Command tomorrow and the money will be given back to you.' But when the poor woman went to the Command the next day nobody knew what money she was referring to. Evidently those two hadn't been Germans at all, just a pair of dishonest rogues. They must have heard that the cashier had taken shelter at our house and thought they would find some money stashed away. They must have taken it for granted that he had stolen from the bank where he had been working, while in fact the poor fellow had taken nothing; he was as honest as the day is long.

As the Allies approached, thousands and thousands of Germans began to pass along the Arno valley. It was more of a rout than a retreat, and there was much confusion. Day after day we saw a constant flow of cars, trucks, cannons and horse-drawn vehicles. If the Germans found someone with a horse and cart they would seize it, put all their possessions into the cart along with anything else they could lay their hands on and drive off. You could hear bombs going off all over the place. The Allies would bomb the railway bridges, the Germans would patch them up again and the Allies would bomb them to pieces yet again. They also bombed the station of San Giovanni, a couple of miles from Montevarchi. They hit a goods train full of petrol, and it went on burning for days. But the Germans gave as good as they got. They had two cannons near the village of Bucine which had a range of nearly twenty miles, which meant that the cannon balls got as far as Florence. Then there was an anti-aircraft battery which shot at the Allied planes. After the bombardments a little aeroplane would appear which was called a *cicogna*. I don't know what its function was, but people said that it was forbidden to fire at it. Perhaps the Germans and the Allies had made an agreement about this. One day, however, the anti-aircraft guns fired at it all the same. After five minutes the Allied bombers came and bombed the battery to pieces.

Then lots of little strips of cellophane began to drift down from the sky like snowflakes, they made me think of those lines from Dante:

Piovean di foco dilatate falde	Large flakes of fire floated down
Come di neve in Alpe senza vento.	Like snow in the Alps when the wind drops.

We would go and pick them up out of curiosity, but we didn't know what they were for. We learnt later that the Allied planes released them to disturb the transmissions between the German telephone lines. And then there were the Bengal lights, the flares launched by the Allied planes at night. They were attached to a sort of parachute and descended very slowly, lighting up the whole countryside. I think they were to show if the Germans were moving their troops in the dark. For us peasants used to oil lamps which would light up an area of about three square feet, these Bengal lights were marvellous things.

One day the Allies got as far as the tower of Galatrona and they began to fire from there with small cannons. They fired towards Mercatale, Rendola, Le Muricce, the *Crocifisso*, places where there were still some Germans. But they didn't come down until they were sure that the Germans had left. They said, 'To make a shell it takes one minute, to make a soldier it takes twenty years.' They could have told Mussolini that when he sent Italian soldiers to Russia ... After a few days a man from Mercatale went up to Galatrona to tell the Allies that the Germans had gone. So they came down to Mercatale and continued their advance.

People began to say, 'The Allies are coming, the Allies are coming!' I was curious to see what these Allies that everybody talked about looked like, so I walked down through the fields towards Mercatale. On the way, near a sort of natural bluff, I saw some English soldiers stretched out behind a tank. They were not afraid of a seventeen-year-old boy barefoot and dressed in rags, as one of them called me and told me to lie down beside them because there were still some Germans around. We heard later that some had gone to Casanova, a farmhouse near the village of Rendola, to say goodbye to the peasants there. They said, 'We'll be back soon!' Apparently they had heard about the V1 and V2, the pilotless planes that were to create so much damage in London, so they thought that these new weapons might halt the advance of the Allies. But thank God, those soldiers never did come back.

Anyway, I spent the afternoon behind that tank with the Allied soldiers. They could speak a little Italian, so I learnt that they were Scottish. I was rather disappointed that they didn't wear kilts as in the pictures I had seen of Scottish people. They wore grey uniforms, but they looked like people on holiday. Some wore vests, others wore shirts, but they all wore shorts. The German and Italian soldiers were always dressed in full uniform with jackets and long trousers, even during the summer. They probably thought that they looked more dignified like that, but they must have been dying with heat wearing all those heavy clothes.

Then one of the soldiers I had made friends with looked at his watch. It was five o'clock in the afternoon. So he pulled out an enamel cup and filled it with water. Then he put a tripod on the ground, stuffed a few dry twigs under it and made a little fire to heat the water for some tea. Thinking I would like it, he offered me a drink. The cup of tea was without sugar and swimming with tea leaves, but I drank it for friendship's sake. So I drank my first cup of tea on the front line!

Later on those soldiers camped in the wood between Mercatale and Rendola near the brick kiln. They slept in tents and kept the lorries close by, because the road was only a hundred yards away. They stayed for about a fortnight. I used to go and visit them, taking them a bottle of *vinsanto* or a basket of fresh eggs, what few things we were able to give them, and they would give me cigarettes and chocolate, which for us were the greatest of luxuries. To reach the camp I had to walk down through the woods from Casa del Bosco. But the Germans hadn't yet left the area and on one occasion I heard a tremendous explosion that made my ears whistle. It was a shrapnel bomb that had gone off quite close, one of those bombs that explodes before it reaches the ground. I was lucky not to have been killed. I realized that it was foolish to leave the house, but boys are foolish and by that time I had got into the habit of visiting my new friends, so I continued to do so in spite of the danger.

Ever since the Armistice we had been able to find out what was happening on our crystal set at home as the news was no longer full of propaganda and lies. We heard that there was a lot of fierce fighting in Florence. Finally the Allies managed to expel the Germans with the help of the anti-Fascists and the war moved slowly northwards, with the Germans resisting all the way. I suppose they just couldn't believe they were losing the war. It would have been better if they had surrendered straightaway and then a lot of lives would have been saved. But the Allies pushed them back and back and when Mussolini saw that the game was up he tried to escape to Switzerland. The partisans caught him and killed him and strung him up in a public square, just like the turkeycock that he was. Soon after, the German army in Italy surrendered and there were celebrations all over Italy. The church bells of Mercatale have never rung so loud and so long! And that was the end of the war as far as Italy was concerned.

When the Allied armies moved towards Florence they left a lot of civil servants to try to bring law and order back to the area. After all, the Allies were now in charge of things, even though they were on our side. So they got to work with the local people to try to get things straight again. War is like a great flood. It leaves so much damage behind that it takes years to get rid of the traces.

The Allies brought us not only cigarettes and chocolate, but also clothes. A fellow used to go round selling military garments by weight. I once bought a shirt and a pair of blue jeans with the letters MP printed on them. They had belonged to the Military Police and when I wore them in Mercatale I created a sensation! I was less lucky with shoes. One day the Allies emptied a lorryful of shoes near Le Muricce and covered them with olive branches. Later other soldiers came to distribute them. I went to see if I could find a pair to fit me, but I found only a shoe for my right foot: they must have hidden shoes for left feet somewhere else, to frustrate would-be thieves like myself. I took the shoe home and kept it on the mantelpiece for months in the hope that I might find its companion. But I never did.

Our main concern was getting enough to eat. Although we had managed to save our oxen, we had very few animals left because the Germans had taken nearly everything. We still had a few sheep, one or two pigs and a dozen hens, but they were not enough to keep a family of six people. Luckily we had had a good harvest, but with all those *sfollati* in the house there were many mouths to feed. Although they all went home after the departure of the Germans, the problem still remained: how would we manage to get through the following winter? In the meantime we picked the grapes and the olives, so that at least we would have wine and oil. But it was the grain we were most worried about: what we had left would not last until the next harvest.

Paciacco, a friend of ours who lived beside the stream in Mercatale and on whose radio we used to listen to Radio Londra, saved the situation. He had a horse and cart and every week he went to San Gusmè, a little village on the other side of the Chianti hills. He would leave the horse and cart in the village and take the bus to Siena in order to go to the market. South of Siena they grew more cereals than in our area and it was easy to find them on the black market. He had established a reliable group of contacts and was able to buy quantities of wheat and have it brought to Mercatale to supply various families there. Normally we would not have had the money to spare, but at that time we were able to earn something. It was the winter of 1944 and in Florence they needed firewood to heat the houses. A fellow called Valentino would buy the timber on a hectare or so of woodland, then we would go and cut it and the Allies would send lorries to take it away. I remember working on the road to Nusenna, and also in Torello's valley. Nobody was frightened of him any longer.

Valentino paid us according to the quantity of wood that we cut and so we had the money to buy grain. They paid us with the money issued by the Allies, as the lira was non-existent at the time. It was the first time we had earned money in exchange for work and it seemed miraculous to us.

What happened to the Fascists? When the Germans had gone they were driven out. Many of them were beaten up. The really worst ones were killed, like Maratti and Pasqualino, but some were not so bad, like the party secretary at Mercatale, and nothing happened to them. However, they were avoided by everybody. If they came to look for oil, for example, no one would give it to them. Then, during the first government formed after the war, Togliatti, the Minister of Justice, and one of the founders of the Communist Party in Italy, declared an amnesty: 'Fascists, Communists, whatever you are, you must stop quarrelling,' he said. 'We have to reconstruct Italy!' He may have been right, but many still felt resentment in their hearts after all the wrongs they had suffered.

We did not feel as afraid of the *padroni* after the war as we used to. It may have been because the Fascists had fallen from power, and many landowners had supported them, in their hearts if not openly. Perhaps, after all the suffering and hardship caused by the war, we all believed that a new world would be created. Perhaps it was because the left-wing political parties, after so many years of repression, began to grow in the fertile ground of the postwar years, like seeds in land that has just been ploughed. We were even less in awe of Groppa Secca: if someone had said that he passed water like anybody else we would no longer have been surprised!

It was during the German retreat that he was dealt a blow which left its mark on him for the rest of his life. His storehouses in Mercatale were crammed with produce: barrels of wine, rows of jars brimming with oil, and dozens of casks of *vinsanto* left there to mature. He didn't need all that stuff but he liked to go

100

and gaze at it as if it were a hoard of treasure, which in a way it was. One day he was crossing the bridge on his way home when the Germans stopped him and forced him to give them the storehouse key. We can imagine with what reluctance the old miser handed it over, but he had no choice. The Germans opened up the storehouse and as they wanted some wine with which to fill up their flasks, they shot at the barrels. All that precious wine began to run out on to the floor, and perhaps the smell was intoxicating because when the Germans had left the people of Mercatale rushed in with bottles to fill them up at the barrels, and they also took away some of the oil and the casks of *vinsanto*, all in front of Groppa Secca. Just imagine! He was the richest and most powerful man in Mercatale who had never made a present of anything to anybody and now he had to put up with this affront. He almost had a heart attack. I would like to say that he became a nicer man after the incident, but it would be a lie. He was mean-hearted right up to his death. But he was more subdued. Perhaps he began to fear those very people whom up until then had always feared him.

CHAPTER 5

A Year in the Life of a *Contadino*

Our family had been reunited since 1943. We were joined by Silvio, the *garzone*, who came from an even poorer family. He was not quite all there, but he actually worked very hard at simple tasks. In those days people like that were expected to work like anybody else. I'm sure that was better for them than shutting them up in mental homes. Silvio would go into the woods with the pigs and if it rained he didn't care how wet he got and he never even got a cold. When he came back he would sit beside the fire with his clothes steaming until they were dry again. He smoked like a chimney, but this didn't seem to have any effect on his health either. Now he's in his seventies and lives at the old folk's home at Montevarchi. Everybody knows him because he walks up and down the main street, begging for cigarette money and picking up fag-ends from the gutters. I think he will die with a cigarette in his mouth!

By the end of the war I was eighteen years old and considered a man now, capable of carrying out all the jobs on the farm alongside my cousin Edoardo and my brother Azeglio. Although society was gradually evolving, there was little change in the daily life of a *contadino* in the years immediately following the war. The country was on its knees and had to be restored to economic health. Changes did eventually come, but slowly. For a while the work went on as usual from the beginning of the year to the end. Season after season there was a never-ending succession of tasks to be carried out: hard work but also the source of great satisfaction. We worked hard, it is true, but we sang as we worked. Nobody sings any more now.

Who knows, some future generation may go back to farming the land: how will they know what to do if I don't explain it to them? So I've described the work of a peasant month by month and, at the beginning of each month is a line of the poem that I know by heart.

JANUARY

Gennaio grandi e piccoli imbacucca . . .
January wraps up warmly old and young alike . . .

In fact, January is the coldest month of the year. We couldn't work much in the fields because they were often frozen hard. It doesn't snow much nowadays, but I remember it used to snow every year and often the snow would remain for weeks on end. We had to dig paths out of the snow, so that you could walk from the house to the woodpile, from the house to the manure heap, from the house to the haystack and the pond, from the house to the spring – three hundred yards of hard shovelling and quite a lot of swearing too. The pond contained rainwater and we used that as drinking water for the animals and for washing our clothes. In the winter it often got covered with a layer of ice ten inches thick, so we had to break the ice every morning with a pick. But firewood was equally important. We needed it not only for heating the kitchen but also for cooking. We also had to warm water for the oxen to drink, as icy water is bad for them. So we used to go out and cut down the scrub oak along the sides of the fields and in the forest. Then we would harness the oxen to the cart and bring the firewood home. They say that firewood warms you up four times: when you cut it, when you load it on to the cart and bring it home, when you carry it into the house and finally when you burn it.

In January we used to go to the chestnut woods to cut poles for the vineyards. In spring you have to replace those that are broken or rotten, and you have to have a pile of new poles ready. First you pick out the straightest trunks, then you cut them down, trim them to the required length, sharpen them at one end, remove the bark and bring them home in the ox cart. I loved working in the woods during the winter. We didn't get cold because the trees sheltered you from the cold winds and we were moving about all the time. When we wanted to have something to eat we would light a little fire, and while we ate, a robin would often fly down to keep us company and share a crumb or two.

All through the winter, of course, we had to feed the animals. We used to cut up turnips for the oxen with the turnip-cutter and mix them up with the chaff. We had to turn the machine by hand and it produced so much dust that it made us cough. Each day we took the sheep and the pigs out, unless there was too much snow on the ground. In the evening we gave the sheep dry leaves, leaves from the branches of poplar and olive that we had prepared for them during the previous months. All the year we had to seek out things for the animals to eat, as we certainly couldn't afford to buy anything. We had to muck them out daily, too, but at least that was a job that kept you warm.

In the winter the days were short, so in the evenings we had time to prepare our tools for the following season. I used to work beside Edoardo in order to learn all sorts of skills. We used chestnut wood to make handles for hoes and spades. We cut it when the moon waned and then we put it aside for a year to season. It became rock-hard and wouldn't break. We used oak wood for the tools we used for the heaviest work: picks, axes and ploughs. For ox yokes we used willow wood, as it was light as well as strong. We made the shelves for the cheeses out of poplar wood because it didn't stain, while for our clogs we used alder wood because it was light and easy to carve. To make a ladder we took a straight chestnut trunk, cut it into two with wedges and then made holes in the two parts for the rungs. We made these out of chestnut wood too, and we forced them into the holes, and then hammered them in to make them fast. We didn't use any nails because we would have had to buy them, and anyway they would have made the wood split. In half a day you could make a ladder that would last for years, without spending a lira. Who knows how many I've made in my time! Now we use aluminium ladders and I do admit that they are nice and light, but when you read about all the pollution man is responsible for, I think ladders made out of chestnut wood are the best. When they get too old to use you can burn them, so they also help to keep you warm.

We didn't work all the time in the winter. We also had fun and

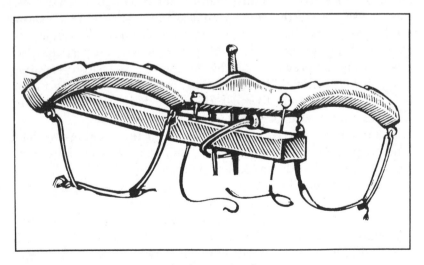

A yoke for a pair of oxen.

when it snowed we couldn't work in the fields anyway. One year the snow was nearly twenty inches deep. All the boys who lived at Le Muricce and nearby got together and one day we said, 'With all this fine snow why don't we make some skis?' In one of our books at school we had seen a picture of some people skiing, but we had never actually seen any skis close up. However, this didn't discourage us. Off we went into the woods to look for the right piece of wood to make skis out of: it had to be wide enough for our feet and have a slight curve. When we found a suitable trunk we brought it home and cooked it in the oven for a while in order to split it more easily. Then we divided it into six pieces and there we were, we had three pairs of skis! All we had to do was to make holes in the pieces of wood and put pieces of wire through them so that we could strap in our clogs, and we were ready to ski. Of course we didn't have any boots, only clogs, and these would fill up with snow, but we didn't care.

By now we were dying to start and nothing could hold us back. From Casino del Monte to the road to Nusenna it was about half a mile and downhill all the way, so it was an excellent ski track and of course we were all champions! We took turns to use the skis, but no one managed to get to the bottom without a fall. Where the road had banks on either side the descent was relatively easy, but where there were no banks we would go shooting off into the olive groves, getting bruises and barked knuckles in the process. It was a miracle that we didn't break any bones. It snowed every day, so we were able to go on skiing for a fortnight or so. The inhabitants of Mercatale began to wait for us on the Nusenna road to see the spectacle and to place bets on whoever got the most bruises. What fun we had, how we laughed, what a lot of tumbles!

When there was snow on the ground my brother Azeglio would follow the tracks of the stoat and the polecat. It would usually snow in the morning and stop in the afternoon, so at dusk the tracks were still visible. He would calculate where they were accustomed to pass and would set a trap with a copper snare. When he managed to catch one of them he would remove the skin by splitting it on either side of the mouth and pulling the whole body through the split. Then he would stuff the skin with corn husks so that it looked alive. But to make a bit of fur to put round one's neck he had to cure the skin, otherwise it would smell.

He used to trap birds as well. There were so many in those days that they were quite a nuisance. They would peck the grapes and the olives and eat up the seed you had just sown. Now the birds are either killed by hunters, or are poisoned by the chemicals the farmers put on the crops, and there are very few left. My brother set traps for them and then roasted them over the fire. He also caught them with birdlime. To make it we used to gather mistletoe berries and put them in a bucket, which we would then cover and put inside the manure heap to boil them. When they were cooked we took them down to the stream to wash them. They were all glued together, but under the water they didn't stick to your hands and when you had washed them several times they formed a kind of skein. We boiled this with a little olive oil and then applied it to the *diavolaccio* with a brush. The *diavolaccio* was a trap in the shape of an umbrella, but without any cloth, and round the ribs there were threads of hemp, so it looked like a spider's web. My brother went round with his trap to the haystacks and the bushes, places where birds would roost for the night. They would try to fly away but they would get caught because of the lime. He brought dozens of these little birds home, and then we would have to kill them and pluck them. With all that lime sticking to them it was hardly worth the effort, in my opinion. There wasn't much flesh on them, but they were considered a treat by most people.

Sometimes my brother managed to catch a hare. Round the fields there were hedges to keep the sheep out and where they were thick you could see where the hare passed because of the fur he left behind. My brother would put a snare on the path and the hare would catch its neck in it. Naturally it was forbidden to catch hare, so we were careful to eat it quickly and give the bones to the dog.

FEBRUARY

Febbraio mette ai monti la parrucca.
February puts a wig on the mountains.

There tended to be less snow in February. It usually melted in our hills but still remained on the top of Pratomagno. But in 1956 the snow came right at the beginning of the month. The weather had been mild, because the rape was already in flower and was two feet high. Then the cold *aretino* began to blow, and a blizzard followed. When it stopped there were ten inches of snow and the ground was frozen at least a foot below the surface. It was bitterly cold even in the house: in my room the urine froze in the chamber pot. The only warm place was the stable. It was important that the oxen should not get cold, so we piled a lot of straw underneath them and kept a pile of manure in the corner which fermented and produced heat. But outside it was terribly cold: the temperature went down to thirteen degrees below freezing and all the birds tried to shelter in the haystacks to escape the cold, poor creatures. My brother caught a lot of them with the *diavolaccio*, but then he stopped. They had got so thin that they were just skin and bone. In the end they died. We found hundreds of bodies in the haystacks and in the holes of trees. A lot of the olive trees died, at least as far as the roots. First all the leaves fell off and then the bark detached itself from the trunk. Afterwards we had to remove the dead trunks and the trees sprouted again from the stump, but those trees produced no olives for a few years. It was a disaster for the peasants, for if they had no oil what could they use for cooking and for dressing their salads?

But usually in February the weather was mild and the days weren't so short. This was when we would start ploughing the land with the oxen. Our soil was heavy and full of clay, so if we ploughed it during the winter the frost might still come and break up the clods. Before ploughing we would put some manure from the manure pit on to the fields. Liquid manure from the stable and from our own lavatory also went into a pit, and we would scoop it out and put it on to the field as well. Round the boles of the olive trees we would put *vermicelli*, strips of rabbit skin which came from the hat factories in Montevarchi. These factories used rabbit skin to make felt hats and the *vermicelli* were the worm-shaped surplus. What with the manure, solid or liquid and the *vermicelli*, we had to handle a lot of strong-smelling stuff and for several days we smelt pretty strongly ourselves.

Everyone talks about organic agriculture nowadays as if it's just been invented, but it seems to me that we used to practise it without making so much song and dance about it. Perhaps because we didn't have much choice anyway.

MARCH

Marzo libera il sol di prigionia . . .
March frees the sun from prison . . .

March was the month we did the pruning. The men pruned the vines and also the field maples which supported them, while the women tied the prunings into bundles to take home and burn on the hearth. We also used them to heat the oven when we baked the bread. Then we pruned the olives. To do this work well you need a lot of skill because each tree is different and needs pruning in a different way. There are not many olive pruners left now and they are all over sixty years old. What will happen when

Pietro prunes the olives.

they die? The bundles of prunings were brought home on the ox cart and put in a heap on the *aia*. By summertime the leaves had dried, so we shook them off to separate them from the wood and gave them to the oxen and the sheep to eat. We didn't throw away the wood, but cut it up to burn. People now burn the prunings in the field, but I must say I hate seeing such good firewood being wasted.

To bind the vines we used willow wands. Willows grow along the streams and the ditches, wherever the ground is damp. You have to cut them before they begin to leaf and lay them in the stream so that they become supple. Some *contadini* still use the willow wands, but unfortunately many use little lengths of plastic now.

We had to work very hard in March because it was the month

we did the sowing. We sowed alfalfa to make hay for the oxen and chickling (a kind of lupin) which was good for the female oxen when they were giving milk, and then we would sow some clover in the field where we had planted corn the preceding autumn: later, when we reaped the corn, the clover would grow in its place. The tradition was to sow potatoes on the last day of Carnival. Then we would sow spring oats, chickpeas, vetch, oats and beans for the oxen and the other animals – and also for ourselves. The oxen ate such a lot and we had to feed them every day even when they didn't work. At least a tractor doesn't consume oil when it is standing in the shed.

Sowing seed is not as easy as you may think. You walk up and down the field with a basket full of seed and you scatter it with a movement of the hand in such a way that you spread it evenly over the ground. If you can't sow well it shows later when the plants grow too close together in one part of the field and there are bare patches in another. If you sowed all day your hand would ache from making that same movement thousands of times. But it was a job that gave you a lot of satisfaction. You must try it to understand that it makes you feel like God! Now people sow with machines, which is much easier and quicker, but the result is that nobody knows how to sow by hand any more, and certainly it isn't as satisfying.

APRIL

Aprile di bei colori orna la via.
April adorns the wayside with lovely colours.

This may be so, but there was so much work to do in April that we had no time to look at the flowers. We had to finish the pruning and the sowing. We sowed the spinach in the vegetable garden, also the onions, the black cabbage, the garlic and the tomatoes. We sowed some salad too, but we ate less of it then than we do now because to make it palatable you have to put olive oil on it and we didn't have much to spare. We tied up the vines, which had already begun to 'weep': the lymph had begun to rise and formed a drop at the end of each stem that had been pruned. Soon the *mignoli*, the olive blossom, would begin to bud. These later would open into greenish-yellow flowers, and when the petals fell off in June you could see the tiny olives. There have to be a lot of buds in April because:

Se mignola di aprile	If the olive blossom buds in April
Vacci col barile,	Get a barrel to collect the oil,
Se mignola di maggio	If the buds come in May
Tanto per l'assaggio,	You'll have just enough to taste,
Se mignola di giugno	If they come in June
Vacci con il pugno.	You'll only get a fistful.

In April you must begin to hoe, hoe, hoe. Everything you have sown that spring has begun to grow, and with it the weeds. So you have to go into the vineyards and dig them out with the *zappa*. You have to remove them also from around the olive trees and everywhere you have sown something, because weeds are right devils, and if they begin to get the upper hand you can't stop them any more. It's a constant battle and you are never sure of winning. Nobody likes working with the *zappa* because after a few hours you get blisters on your hands, however tough your skin is, and your back begins to ache, as you have to work bending down. However, you have to go on digging, otherwise those damned weeds will suffocate everything you have sown.

In April we also had to attend to the silkworms because the mulberry trees had begun to produce leaves and those are what the silkworms live on. The *padrone* gave us the eggs (he bought them by the ounce from the chemist), and the women kept them in their bosoms wrapped in pieces of cloth until the caterpillars hatched. Then they put them on *castelli*, reed mats supported by a wooden frame. There was one in each bedroom and every day they were fed with leaves stripped from the mulberry: I remember clambering up the tree even when I was a small boy and cutting down the smaller branches. Gradually the caterpillars grew, until the moment came to 'send them to the wood'. We propped some tree heather against the wall and they climbed up to make their cocoons, which were about the size of peanuts. When the cocoons were ready we took them down in a basket to the market in Montevarchi. But we didn't earn very much because we had to give half of what they gave us to the *padrone*.

In April it rains frequently and then the sun comes out. We say: '*Aprile, quando piange e quando ride*' – 'April, one moment she weeps and the next she smiles.' With this kind of weather parasites appear very easily, for example, the *peronospora* which everyone fears. So then we had to start spraying the vines. We would fill a barrel with water and then put in some lumps of copper sulphate, together with a little lime. We would stir it all up to get rid of the lumps: then we would pour some of it into copper spraying machines, strap them on to our backs and walk up and down the vines spraying them by working a handle back and forth. This made a creaking noise, so if somebody was doing the spraying it was easy to find them even if they were quite far away. We had to spray the olives too, otherwise they would also get diseased. It was tiring work because you had to fill up the machine frequently and it was a job you did three or four times a year, even more often if the weather was warm and humid. Now they do the same job using a tractor, which saves a lot of labour.

MAY

Maggio vive fra musiche d'uccelli . . .
May is alive with birdsong . . .

It is true, all the birds sing in May: the robins, the blackbirds, the wrens, the nightingales, the hoopoes and the golden orioles. The orioles always used to fly into the fig trees. The male would wait on the bank and call: '*E' pronto il fico?*' 'is the fig-tree ready?' and the female would reply, '*Che, che, che!*' Then the male would ask, '*C'è pericolo?*' 'is there any danger?' and the female would reply, '*Che, che, che!*' Then the peasant would shoot at them and they would both fly off crying, '*C'è pericolo, c'è pericolo!*' It really sounds as if they are saying these words. Now you hardly ever see an oriole – they have all been killed by the poison farmers put in the fields. The hoopoe used to be common too, and nowadays we see only a few of them every season.

In May we had to make hay for the oxen. We called it the first cut, and it was a mixture of alfalfa and other grasses. The second cut took place at the end of June, and was made up mostly of alfalfa, like the third cut, which if we were lucky took place in September. But the first cut was the most plentiful. We used to cut the hay with scythes. We would leave the hay lying on the ground for two or three days, and then we would turn it over so that the part that had been in contact with the ground would dry as well. When that was dry we would put the hay in heaps, then take it back to the *aia* to make a stack. The proverb goes: '*Maggio ombroso ma non piovoso,*' 'May is cloudy but not rainy,' but actually it did rain quite often. Once the hay had got wet it deteriorated, going brown instead of green, and sometimes it would get a little mouldy, but we would have to bring it in all the same. To make a stack we would put the loose hay round a pole, and when it was high enough we would thatch it with straw in

115

the shape of a cone. Making a haystack was quite an art as you had to make sure that the rain didn't get in and spoil the hay.

In May we used to wash the sheep and shear them. We took them down to the Tricesimo at Mercatale and threw them one by one into the water, something they didn't like at all. One person would do the throwing, two others would hold the sheep and wash it: you had to squeeze the fleece all over its body to get the dirt out and then you let the sheep go and dry in the sun. We had only about twenty sheep, so with a morning's work we managed to wash them all. Then we took each one, tied its legs together, put it up on the cart and sheared it. We gave half the fleeces to our *padrone*, the other half we kept ourselves. The women used to spin the wool themselves, until the fifties, when they would take it down to a fellow called Marcello down in Montevarchi (he's still alive). He had machines that would spin and weave the wool, so he could give us the cloth ready to be made up into clothes.

JUNE

Giugno ama la frutta appesa ai ramoscelli.
June loves the fruit hanging on the branches.

In June the cherries were ready, but most of the fruit, for example, the apples, pears, figs, apricots and plums, were not ripe yet. We had to wait until autumn to pick them.

This was the month that everything grew and it was very satisfying. We would try to get ahead with all the work on the farm so that we could dedicate the following month to the most tiring task of all: the harvest. We went on digging out the weeds as that was a never-ending job, and we worked in the vegetable garden, earthing up the potatoes and removing the weeds there too. Then we had to look after the vines. In June they produced a lot of foliage, and we had to remove most of that so that the sun could reach the grapes which were just beginning to swell. We gave the cuttings to the pigs and the oxen. We had to spray sulphur on to the grapes to kill the pests. Then we would spray the vines with copper sulphate, the olives, too, if it was necessary.

But now the weather was getting hot, so we would start work very early in the morning, about half past four. During the hot part of the day we would have a siesta. Of course we went around barefoot, nobody wore clogs from March onwards. Your feet used to get hard, you could even walk on stones without feeling anything.

Talking about bare feet, I'll tell you a true story. At that time of year the peasants would often stop working at about eleven o'clock because of the heat, and they would then go along to the smith to have their tools sharpened. Often a group formed, and they would have a good gossip while they waited for their turn. One day, as they stood there, they could smell something burning, like when you roast meat. They kept asking themselves what it could be, but they couldn't work out where the smell was coming from. What had happened was this: the smith had just made a billhook and he had thrown it down to cool so that he could sharpen it later. Begna, one of the peasants (he was the father of Quirino, the fellow who ate the earthworms), had stepped on the red-hot billhook with his heel, and the skin was burning; but it was so thick that he couldn't feel it, it was the others who discovered he was burning. They said: 'Begna, you're burning!' He hadn't felt a thing.

One day this same Begna went into his cellar at midday to draw off a flask of wine. As usual he locked the door behind him when he went away. In the evening he went back for another flask of wine but he couldn't find the key, so the family had to go without wine for supper. Then he went to bed, and when he took off his clogs he found the key inside one of them. Probably he had meant to put it into his waistcoat pocket, but it had slipped down a trouser-leg and into his clog. He had been walking round all the afternoon without realizing the key was there, and it was a big one, as thick as your finger!

JULY

Luglio falcia le messi al solleone . . .
July reaps the harvest under the hot sun . . .

At Casa del Bosco we had four hectares of corn to reap: it grew between the rows of vines and also among the olives. In those days we didn't waste an inch of ground because we used the corn to make bread with and we ate a great deal in a year. The whole family came out to reap the corn with sickles. A fellow called Marzilino came to help us, as he didn't have any land of his own. We worked even on Sundays, when friends came along to help us as well as other agricultural workers. We worked in a line, each one had a strip to reap, and when we reached the end of a field wuie would drink some water and then set off in the opposite direction. If the corn was still rather green we would spread it out to dry in the sun. If it was already dry we would tie it into bundles with a length of straw. After a few days we gathered the bundles together and made a stook, in such a way that all the ears of corn were in the middle. Then we would arrange the day of the threshing. Several people owned threshing machines in the area: Papini of Montevarchi, Sacconi who lived near Ambra, Leonello of Nusenna. On the appointed day we would go into the field with the ox cart and bring the corn to the *aia*. We didn't do it earlier because of the risk of fire.

About thirty or forty people gave a hand to thresh the corn because there was so much work, and once the threshing machine was set in motion it didn't stop till the job was finished. We untied the bundles and threw them into the machine and then the corn would come out at the back and we would have to put it into

Threshing.

sacks. Half of these were for our family and half for Groppa Secca, and he was always present to check that the corn was shared out equally (in other words, that we didn't pinch a sack or two). The straw came out separately and that had to be put into stacks. Then there were the husks, the parts of the ear of corn that surrounded the grain. We raked those together and put them into a special stack, surrounded by bamboo canes and with a roof made out of tree heather. We gave that to the sheep during the winter. All that was left was the *pagliolo*, the leaves on the straw stalks, and we put that aside to mix into the feed of the oxen. It didn't have much nutritive value. In fact, if you saw an ox that looked on the skinny side you would ask the peasant, 'What did you feed him on during the winter, *pagliolo*?' However, we wasted nothing. Only dust was left.

So we worked round the threshing machine for three or four hours, the time it took to thresh the corn of a medium-sized farm. If you had the first shift you began at half past three in the morning, but if you had a later shift you often had to work in the heat of the day. It was exhausting work, with all the heat and the noise and the dust. The women didn't participate because they had to prepare the food for all those people. But the work didn't finish there, because after you had threshed your own corn you had to go and help other peasants to thresh theirs and there were about thirty farms in the area. All the peasants helped one another. It was impossible to do the work with only one family as you needed many pairs of hands. Working clothes were very heavy in those days, goodness how we sweated! No one dreamed of taking off his shirt as people would do nowadays. And yet we had a lot of fun, we shouted and sang and joked, and then we all ate together and had a merry time. This went on all July – by August we had just about finished.

When we took our sacks of corn into the house we emptied them on to the floor of a room on the first floor so that the corn wouldn't get damp. Then we had to treat it with sulphur, otherwise it would get mites. We put a cane into the middle and poured sulphur down it, then we closed the door and the windows. In this way it wouldn't spoil. It was very satisfying indeed to see that heap of corn and we would then feel ready to face the following winter.

AUGUST

Agosto, avaro, ansando le ripone.
Miserly August, panting, stores the grain.

To tell the truth, we did not store the grain in August because we had usually finished the harvest by the end of July. This rhyme was written in another part of Tuscany, in the Maremma, perhaps, where the fields of corn are much bigger than in our area, so the harvest-time goes on for longer. In fact a great number of farm-workers used to go to the Maremma to work. Before it had been drained it was an unhealthy area and they would often come back with malaria. Maybe you have heard the song '*Maremma amara*', 'Cruel Maremma', where a woman mourns the death of her husband, struck by malaria when he was helping with the harvest:

Tutti mi dicono Maremma Maremma,	Everyone says to me Maremma Maremma,
E a me mi pare una Maremma amara,	To me it seems a cruel Maremma,
L'uccello che ci va perde la penna,	The bird that goes there loses a feather,
Io ci ho perduto una persona cara,	I lost my beloved there,
Sia maledetta Maremma Maremma . . .	A curse on you, Maremma Maremma . . .

As soon as the grain harvest was over we had to harvest the chickpeas, the broad beans, the beans, the chickling and the vetch. The first two were for us, the others for the animals. We made piles in the fields and when the plants were dry we brought them to the threshing-floor and threshed them with a tool called a *correggiato*. A *correggia* is a fart, so you can imagine what kind of noise it made!

In August we had to clear the fields and prepare them for the next season. First we had to plough the land where the corn had been harvested. We harnessed the oxen to the plough and ploughed really deep, as much as a foot. In this way we brought the roots of all the weeds to the surface and they would wither. Then we would dig up the banks between one field and the next, so that the plants growing there would not invade the cultivated land. Afterwards we would rake together all the dried-up weeds and make *fornelli*, little ovens, out of them: we would cover the heaps with earth and then burn them. This 'cooked' the earth and where you spread it more grain would grow.

After this operation we would plough the fields again and prepare them for sowing the wheat. We didn't do this until October, but we had to prepare the fields a long time before. We also ploughed the land where the beans and so on had been harvested, but without ploughing too deep, because when you plough the land it must either be very wet or very dry, otherwise nothing grows there.

In August we also cleaned out the ponds. These were holes in the ground that we had created to hold the rainwater: the spring was a long way away, so these ponds were very useful and were to be found all over the farm. One pond was specially for white lime: we would buy some lumps and put them in the pond, then the water would bubble and there you had your lime. We used to mix it with the copper sulphate and spray it on the vines and olives so that the liquid would stick to the leaves. In another pond we used to soak the acorns for the pigs. In the summer the ponds would dry up, so we could deepen them and remove the weeds inside them before the rains came in autumn. We also used to dig out the ditches that carried the rainwater to the ponds.

Pietro with his oxen.

Nobody looks after the ponds and ditches any longer which is why there are so many floods and landslides. In the past the peasants used to try to retain the water, but now it all runs down the hillsides, with the results that we all know about.

In the spring we used to cut some fresh grass with the sickle for the oxen, but by August there was none left. So we cut branches off the oak trees in the woods, brought them home and stripped them of their leaves. We would mix these into the feed for the oxen. We tried not to give them any hay because we needed that for the winter. We used to give poplar leaves to the sheep: there were a lot of poplar trees down by the stream and we used to climb up them and remove the branches with a hook. To avoid climbing up and down too often my brother Azeglio would go to the top of tree and make it sway until he could jump to the next tree: he did this fifty feet from the ground, so he risked killing himself, but he was as agile as a monkey and never fell. We brought the branches home in the ox cart.

SEPTEMBER

A settembre ci sono i bei grappoli a rubini . . .
In September there are the ruby-coloured grapes . . .

Before the wine-harvest we went to the chestnut woods to clear the undergrowth round the *marroni* trees. I had seven little pieces of woodland, the ones left to the Bigoli family by Torello the priest. We cut down all the brambles, and cleared the ground under those trees so well that if you'd lost a pin you'd have been able to find it. Then we dug out little trenches so that when we beat the chestnuts they wouldn't bounce too far down the hillside. While we did this work we often found a *porcino* mushroom or two, and these would be a special treat for supper that night. Then we prepared poles out of chestnut wood, neither too heavy nor too long, and used them for knocking the chestnuts off the higher branches. We took the poles home and cooked them in the oven so that we could take off the bark more easily and make them lighter, stronger and more flexible.

Now the grape harvest was approaching, so we had to prepare everything for that too. First we used to make the baskets for gathering the grapes. We used chestnut saplings, the ones that were straight and smooth. We cooked them and then soaked them to make them more flexible. When they had softened we shaped them with a knife designed for the purpose. This required precision, it was an art, really. With the strips we would make baskets of all shapes and sizes: there were no plastic containers in those days. We made baskets to carry the firewood in, to gather grass for the rabbits, to collect the eggs, for picking olives and chestnuts, for taking the silkworm cocoons down to the market and so on. I knew someone who made baskets so well that you could fill them with water and they wouldn't lose a drop.

Then we would have to make the *scalei*, pointed ladders. We took a chestnut trunk and split it, but not right to the top. We would put a ring of iron round the top to stop it splitting further and then we slowly pulled the two halves apart and connected them with rungs. These were too narrow for your foot at the top, so they would stick out at the sides. We used this kind of ladder to climb on to the field maples that supported the vines. They would stay in place better than normal ones.

When the harvest began we would first choose the grapes for the *governo*, and also for the *vinsanto*. We chose the best bunches and laid them carefully in special open baskets. We took ten baskets home and gave ten to the *padrone*. The women used to carry the baskets on their heads, because if we had put them on the ox cart the grapes would have been shaken about and bruised. Then we placed the bunches with care on reed matting suspended on a wooden frame and left them there until November.

Every evening we went down to the room where the vats were kept and with the machine we used for spraying the vines we sprayed the vats with water. This was to make the wood swell, otherwise the vats wouldn't hold the wine. We did this every evening for a couple of weeks, and then we began the harvest, at the end of September or the beginning of October, depending on the weather. At Casa del Bosco we hadn't a great quantity of grapes, so it took us only four or five days to pick them. The whole family took part to make it quicker, and we joked and laughed a lot because it was easy work. Now and then we used to pop a grape or two into our mouths to check that it was good – or so we said. We took the oxen to the vineyard with a small vat on top of the cart. We emptied our baskets into a *bigone*, a container about waist-high made of wooden staves, and then we used a stick with a thickened end to crush the grapes inside it. After that we emptied the *bigone* into the vat on the ox cart and stamped the grapes down with our bare feet. When the vat was full we took it to Mercatale and used the *bigoni* to empty the grapes into the big vats there. When a vat was full, we would tread the *vinaccia*, the mass formed by the skins and stems of the grapes, down into the vat; because if it stayed on the surface the wine would turn to vinegar. But we only did this when the vat was full, because if your head was not above the top of the vat you could be overcome by the fumes, and that happened from time to time. The wine fermented and was hot, if you had rheumatism in your legs it would cure you, and it was also a good way of getting your feet clean . . . So we continued to tread on the grapes, until after about ten days the wine would stop fermenting and it was time to remove it from the vats. We fixed a tap at the bottom of the vat and removed the wine. By this time it was clear and almost drinkable. We would put the wine into small barrels containing fifty litres each: the first ten for the *padrone*, the next ten for us, the next ten for the *padrone* and so on. Then we would take the barrels back to our own cellar on the ox cart. We could carry ten barrels at a time, so we had to make several journeys. We emptied the barrels into the larger ones and didn't touch the wine again until November.

As for the *vinaccia*, a sort of purple mass by now, we pressed it in a machine made for the purpose, and put what came out into a separate barrel. This wine would have a stronger colour than usual, but it was excellent. We certainly didn't throw anything away! We also distilled the lees and made some grappa. I've never tasted better. We did that secretly because it was forbidden to make it by law, but we lived close to the woods and the law never came our way.

September was the month for fruit: we had apples, pears, peaches and figs. My mother used to make *picce* with the figs: she removed the skin and then put them on a *graticcio*, a frame made of chestnut wood and wild clematis stems woven together, to dry in the sun. When they were dry she split them, put some aniseed inside and then closed them up again. She then wrapped the *picce* in a piece of paper with a bay leaf inside so that the mites wouldn't get in. Finally she tied up the pieces of paper with willow twigs and put them away for the winter. There were no sweets in those days, or if there were we couldn't have afforded them, so the figs prepared in this way were a real treat. I adored them because I love sweet things. If I eat too many now it's because I had so few when I was a child.

This was the month when my mother would make the tomato sauce. She put the tomatoes on *graticci* and put them into the oven after baking the bread. When they were cooked she took them out and pressed each one with her finger to remove the juice. Next she passed them through a sieve to remove the skins and the seeds and then boiled them very slowly with some salt. When most of the liquid had boiled away she poured the rest into jars and put a little olive oil on top before closing them. In this way she would have enough tomato sauce to cook with until the following spring.

OCTOBER

Ottobre di buon mosto riempe i tini.
October fills the vats with good must.

We picked the grapes either at the end of September or at the beginning of October, depending on the weather: if it was very sunny the grapes ripened earlier, if September was cloudy we would wait to see if there was going to be more sun in October. But if it rained a lot we would have to pick the grapes all the same, otherwise they would go mouldy. Sometimes we beat the chestnuts before the grape harvest. The problem was this: if we went first to beat the chestnuts someone would steal our grapes, while if we picked the grapes first someone would steal our chestnuts, we lost out whatever happened! It was the *pigionali*, the people paying rent for their houses, who stole things. They had no land and had to survive somehow.

The whole family went to beat the chestnuts. We used the poles we had already prepared to knock them down, or we climbed up the trees. It was a dangerous job because the trees were up to sixty feet tall and each year some beaters fell and hurt themselves. Some were actually killed. The women's task was to rake the chestnuts together and take them to the *ricciaia*, a deep pit that we used from year to year. There was a fence round it and we would cover the chestnuts in their husks (the *ricci*) with branches of juniper and tree heather to protect them from the pigs – and also from human beings. Then we would leave them there to soften up until the end of October.

There were three beaters in our family: Edoardo, Azeglio and myself. But many peasants had so many chestnuts that they couldn't manage to beat them themselves, for example, the peasants at Sinciano, the village in the hills above Mercatale. So at the end of September they went to the Terranuova fair, the biggest fair in the Arno valley. There they would hire some young folk from Pratomagno, even from the Casentino on the other side of the mountain, and they would fix a day to go all together to the chestnut woods. The young men would do the beating, the women would rake up the chestnuts, there were often thirty or so young folk working together and you could hear them chatting and singing from far away. In the evening they would go to the peasant's house and dance before going to bed. It was a merry time and one of the few occasions that young people could meet others from a different area, because even Pratomagno on the other side of the Arno valley seemed a long distance away and those living there had a different dialect. Friendships were formed, and several of the young people became engaged on the spot.

In October we had to start sowing the wheat. We sowed it all over the place, not only in the fields set aside for the purpose, but also among the vines and the olives. We sowed above all by hand.

Later on Groppa Secca bought three sowing machines which we could harness the oxen to, but as there were three of them and there were seven farms all needing them at the same time, we were often unable to use them. At Casa del Bosco sowing was always a worry because the ground was full of clay. There was not much that was suitable for growing wheat and if we didn't manage to sow enough we would not have enough flour to last a year.

At the end of the month we went back to the chestnut woods to deal with the chestnuts. We would uncover them and use a special tool to separate the nuts from the husks (just try touching those husks, they are full of prickles!). Then we would rake up the chestnuts into a separate pile, put them into sacks and take them home in the ox cart. We couldn't leave the sacks in the wood, otherwise they would be stolen by the *pigionali*. Those unfortunate people would search the woods for any chestnut we might have left behind. Just think how poor those people were, walking a mile or two in the hills for a handful of chestnuts.

When we got home we emptied the sacks on to the floor of one of the rooms and sorted out the chestnuts. Naturally the *padrone* took half of them. We asked a carter to take our best ones down to Montevarchi for us, and there we sold them at the market. The ones with maggots we gave to the pigs, but we ate the rest. We roasted them in the fire or boiled them with fennel and salt. It was hard work getting those chestnuts in, but we forgot about that when the moment came to eat them, they were so delicious.

NOVEMBER

Novembre ammucchia aride foglie in terra . . .
November gathers the dead leaves into heaps . . .

In November we had to finish sowing the wheat, as the proverb advises:

A Year in the Life of a Contadino

Quando s'arriva ai Santi	When All Saints' Day arrives,
La semina dev'essere	The sowing must be
Mezza indietro e mezza avanti.	Half completed and half to be done.

But we had to finish by the eleventh:

Per San Martino	After St Martin's Day
E' la sementa del pigherino.	Only the lazy man still has to sow.

This was because November is a rainy month and it is hard to sow when the ground is very wet.

After the sowing we would do the *governo* of the wine. I have learnt since that this takes place only in Tuscany. That's why we have the best wine in the world! We took the bunches of grapes which we had selected before the grape harvest and removed the stems and the seeds. Then we threw the grapes into the barrels through a little door at the top specially made for the purpose. The wine would ferment again for about ten days and would gain in colour and strength. If the wine did not have enough colour we would first put the grapes for a while in the oven, and this would improve the colour of the wine. Sometimes we put whole bunches inside the barrels. Then, when we drew off the wine these bunches would still be intact and they were quite delicious.

After the second fermentation we cemented a *colmatore*, or cask-filler, into the top of each barrel. This apparatus contained water and would let the vapours escape without permitting air to enter the barrel, otherwise the wine would turn to vinegar. It would also indicate if the level of the wine went down, in which case you had to top it up again. Then we left the wine to mature until the spring. Before the hot weather came we put the wine into another barrel, otherwise the lees would alter the taste. We drew off a flask or two every time we needed it, and left the rest there until the autumn. Then we put what was left in demijohns and sold it to dealers or shopkeepers. But often we kept it for ourselves, because even though we put water into it when we drank it there was barely enough for the family.

We used the rest of the grapes we had set apart to make *vinsanto*. Red grapes or white, it didn't matter. We would crush it in the *bigoni* and then we took it to Gretole where they had a machine for squeezing out the rest of the juice. We put the juice in a small cask and cemented it up at once, otherwise it would explode when it fermented. We usually opened up the flask to drink the wine at threshing-time, but the longer you left it the better. We didn't usually sell our *vinsanto*, we kept it for feast days to offer to our relations. Everyone tried to produce better *vinsanto* than anybody else – there was quite a lot of rivalry! Sometimes we put a bit of honeycomb in it to give it a special aroma, or else two or three twigs of juniper. We used to make vermouth too. We took some must made of white grapes and put some spices in it (we would buy these from the chemist). Then we put it in flasks and later removed it with an apparatus called a *tromba da vino*, to avoid disturbing the lees. We used to dip biscuits into it when we had guests, but we never drank it when the family was alone.

Now the olive harvest was approaching and we had to prepare for it. We mended the baskets and ladders or made new ones and cleared the ground round the olive trees of brambles and other weeds. We picked up the olives that the wind had already blown off the trees. Then we got the firewood ready, because as soon as we started picking we wouldn't have time to go to the woods. The first cold spells came in November and we would see the first snow on the top of Pratomagno. We had to prepare for winter, no peasant would relax until he had a good pile of firewood on the *aia*. So we cut the scrub oak along the edges of the fields or in the wood and we also removed quite a lot of wood from the olive trees; because when they are old the inner part of the trunk dies and you have to remove it with a tool called a *malinpeggio*. Then we collected the acorns and put them in a pond to rot. Later we would give them to the pigs to fatten them and give the meat a better flavour.

DECEMBER

Dicembre ammazza l'anno e lo sotterra.
December kills the year and buries it.

We began to pick the olives at the beginning of December. Locally it was said that you shouldn't start picking until the feast day of Caposelvi, that is, the eighth of the month. Then there is a proverb which says:

Per Santa Lucia	For St Lucy's Day
Lascia la ghianda e prendi l'ulia.	Leave the acorns and pick the olives.

St Lucy's Day was 13 December, but we had over a thousand trees, so when there was a good crop we had to start at the end of November. First we prepared the wood for the olive press. When Groppa Secca gave the order, all his peasants met in the woods and the woodman told us which trees we could cut down. We hewed away all day and by the evening we had a large quantity of firewood. We took this down to the olive press in the ox cart. The wood was needed to boil the water in the boiler and also to warm the room, otherwise the oil would not come out of the olives. When all this was done we could start to pick. The men climbed up the trees on ladders with their baskets strapped round their necks to free their hands, while the women picked the olives off the lower branches, and also gathered those that had fallen to the ground. Perhaps the women didn't climb the ladders in case the men looked up their skirts! But it is true that it was more dangerous work, because if the ladder slipped you could fall and break a shoulder. But the most tiring work was picking the olives off the ground, because you had to bend down and your hands got cold from touching the damp ground. While picking grapes is a merry business, nobody enjoyed picking olives much because of the cold; sometimes the north wind would blow but you had to go on picking before the first frosts came, otherwise the olives would get 'cooked'. They would get all wrinkled and the oil would not be so good.

Olive-picking

We put the olives in sacks and emptied them into a room in the house, spreading them out so that they wouldn't get crushed. When there was a certain quantity we would sack them up again. We would do this using a *bigone*: this contained twenty-five kilos and we would have to take the equivalent of sixty-four full *bigoni* to the olive press, which was the amount we could press in two days. We didn't work at night, only during the day: 'The night is for sleeping,' Groppa Secca would say. It would appear that he was thinking of the peasants' welfare, but actually it was because he wanted to go and sleep himself and if we went on working he couldn't keep an eye on us. In other olive presses they worked all night and finished sooner. They didn't have Groppa Secca for *padrone*.

We started work at six in the morning, when it was still dark. We heated the water in the boiler and lit the fire on the hearth. Then we carried the sacks of olives – they weighed fifty kilos each! – to the first floor of the building and poured the olives into a *tramoggia*, a kind of giant funnel made of wood. From there the olives would drop down a tube on to the millwheels. These were inside a thick circular stone with a metal rim almost three feet high and went round and round grinding the olives. All this was powered by electricity, but before the war some millwheels were turned by a blindfolded donkey walking in a circle.

When the olives were ground they formed a thick paste. This was poured on to the *gabbie*, which were big circular disks made of thick matting. We carried these over to the hydraulic press and put under it eight or nine of them one on top of the other. Then, under the supervision of the *frantoiano*, the man in charge of the whole operation, four men activated the press and gradually the olive oil came out and flowed into a tub. This was the first pressing and about half of the oil would be produced. Then we would press the *gabbie* a second time to get the rest of the oil out. The first process was called *oliva*, the second *mezz-oliva*, but the oil was all of the same quality and was mixed together. Then we emptied another load of olives into the funnel and started again, until all the olives were converted into oil. In one day we would repeat the operation sixteen times. For us peasants used to being in the open air, the long hours spent in the press were torture. In addition, the new oil had a heavy, pungent smell. I love putting olive oil on my food but I used to get a violent headache from breathing in that smell all those hours in the press.

At six o'clock in the evening the *padrone* supervised while the *frantoiano* and the *contadini* present transferred the oil (the water by this time had sunk to the bottom) into small barrels and emptied these into large, shallow earthenware *vasche*. The oil was left there for a few days for the sediment to form. In the meantime one of the women prepared supper in the room where the pressing took place. When we were ready to eat Groppa Secca would turn to one of the peasants and say in that weak little voice that made him sound always on the point of death, 'Could you check to see whether I've locked all the doors?' So we had to wait for the peasant to come back. Sometimes he would find a door unlocked, but Groppa Secca had probably left it unlocked on purpose to see whether the peasant was checking the doors properly. And if a door was unlocked Groppa Secca would strike himself on the forehead as if to say, 'What a careless fellow I am!' and go off with the bunch of keys to lock the door. Then he would go away, but in the meantime our supper had got cold. I'm convinced he did it on purpose. We had to eat up quickly because the *frantoiano* had to lock the street door and take the key to the *padrone* before he went to bed.

On the second day we made the *olio di sansa*. At six o'clock in the morning we once again heated up the boiler and boiled the water. Then we took the *sansa*, the paste that was left over on the *gabbie* from the day before, added hot water to it and ground it again. Then we put the paste on to the *gabbie* and put them under the press. It took a lot of effort to squeeze some more oil out but finally we managed it. This oil was of inferior quality to the oil we had made the day before and we kept it separate. We used it in the family because nobody wanted to buy it.

I often see olive oil on sale on the big farms and the price is very high. They sell it in small bottles so that the purchaser (usually a foreigner) has the impression he isn't spending very much. But if you make a simple calculation, that oil costs up to forty thousand lire (about twenty Euros) a litre, an excessive sum. The farmers say that the price is high because the oil is produced during the first pressing: 'Look, it's written on the label!' But all olive oil on the market (except for the *olio di sansa*, which very few people use now) is produced in the first pressing, even in the more modern presses. The quality of the oil depends purely on the degree of acidity: the less there is the better the oil. The 'extra virgin oil', for example, mustn't have more than 0.3 per cent acidity. But forty thousand lire a litre is a dishonest price, in my opinion, whatever the quality of the oil. Of course, it may be the price of labour nowadays that pushes up the prices.

In a good year we used to make the olive oil four or five times, and often we didn't finish until New Year's Eve or even Epiphany, on the sixth of January. Each time we would bring back home our share of the oil and store it in earthenware jars. After so much hard work it was a great pleasure to pour that new oil on to a piece of bread. When it was just made the oil was dense and green and had such a peppery taste that it would make your throat burn.

Another great pleasure at that time of year was eating fresh pork. We would kill a pig before Christmas so that we would have more meat for the feast days. On the established day the *norcino* used to come with all his apparatus. He killed the pig and cleaned it with the help of the women of the house (the men were still busy with the olives). Then he cut the pig into pieces and put them on the table, on the benches, on the *madia*, wherever there was some space. He would keep the cheek, the bacon, the shoulders and the hams separate from the rest, to cover with salt and spices later on, while the ribs and the trotters were put inside the *madia* to eat on the following days, otherwise they would go bad. Then he minced the rest of the meat and made sausages, *salame* and *finocchiona*. He would make *capaccia* from the head, ears and skin, while the *burischio* was made from the blood. He wouldn't waste a scrap! Nowadays people would refuse to eat some parts of the pig, but we were hungry and even the *burischio* was a treat in our eyes.

We sold the other fattening pigs and shared out the earnings with Groppa Secca. We kept back, however, some sows to produce sucking pigs and sent them off into the woods to eat acorns, which were still to be found until the end of March.

And so the year was well and truly buried. We had worked hard but there had been many rewards. And another year was about to start, exactly similar to the one that preceded it. But it never even occurred to us that we might change our way of life: '*Chi ha zolle stia con le zolle*,' 'he who has clods should remain with the clods,' as the saying goes, and we believed it.

Yet, of those peasants who worked the land up to the sixties very few are left. Many have died, others have gone to live in the town. Only a few managed to buy their *poderi* when the opportunity arose and have become farmers in their own right. But their children, instead of following in their father's footsteps, have sought work from some other *padrone*. So, in the space of twenty years, a whole world has vanished.

CHAPTER 6

Pastimes and Feast Days

We worked hard all the year round. We took it for granted that life was hard, and perhaps for that reason it was less hard: we envisaged no alternative. And it is undeniable that most of us enjoyed our work and drew a lot of satisfaction from it. We were always happy to see the fat and glossy oxen standing knee-deep in straw in the stable, the barrels of wine and the jars of olive oil in the cellar, the heap of wheat in a room on the first floor, the tomatoes and maize hanging from the balcony.

But life was not all hard work: we had moments of fun and relaxation too. Every evening, for example, there was the *veglia*, when the whole family gathered round the fire. We could all relax after the day's labour, though usually our hands were still busy: the women would spin, the men would mend baskets or make new handles for their tools. Often a neighbour would drop in and make his contribution to the company.

The men used to play cards, but the women didn't, they were too busy spinning or knitting. I never saw women playing cards, it was not the custom. Sometimes they played *cruschello*. They would put a heap of *crusca*, or bran, on the table and everyone would put a coin inside. Someone would mix the coins into the bran to hide them and then each player would take a little heap. Anyone who found a coin in his heap could keep it.

We often used to tell stories, funny or otherwise. The men would vie with each other to see who could tell the best one. This was one of my favourite stories. After the war a couple of Italians left the country to work in Belgium. When they came back they both tried to tell the tallest story. Said one: 'Let me tell you, the cabbages there are huge! I saw one in the middle of a field that was so big that five hundred sheep could shelter in its shade!' Whereupon the other one said: 'That's nothing, my friend! Where I was living they made enormous cooking pots. There was one that was so big that there were twenty-five smiths hammering away inside it and none of them could hear the blows the others were making!' One of the listeners was puzzled. 'But what could be the use of such a big cooking pot?' 'That's simple,' said another, who was more sceptical, 'to cook our friend's cabbage in!'

The women didn't usually tell stories as they were less willing to draw attention to themselves. They were more interested in health problems, which could be resolved by visiting a wise woman. If you had a boil, for example, the wise woman would touch it with her ring and say some magic words, very quickly and under her breath, otherwise you could learn them too. After a couple of days the boil would either shrink or come to a head and burst (as would have happened anyway, in my opinion, without the help of the wise woman). If on the other hand a child got a sore throat, people used to say he had worms and the mother would go to Gina, a wise woman who lived in Starda, to get rid of them. She would put two or three hemp threads in a glass of water and stir them round, uttering a spell. Then she would take them out and say, 'Now the worms have gone, I've got rid of them!' And the mother would give her a coin and go back home satisfied that her child was cured.

Some of these wise women healed you, others were real witches who cast evil spells on you. They secretly stole a couple of hairs off your head and used them to tie a toad to a bush. As the toad grew weaker and weaker you got more and more seriously ill, and when the toad died you followed him to the other world. The only way to save you was to free the toad before it was too late, but who could find it?

I must admit I didn't believe in these superstitions, and yet, to be on the safe side, I used to nail a branch of pine to my front door. It was said that, before entering, a witch was obliged to count all the pine needles. This would take such a long time that in the end she would lose patience and go away.

There weren't only wise women and witches around, there were also wizards. If you had a mysterious illness you went to a wizard. The further away he lived the more likely it was that he could cure you. One day a girl fell ill and her temperature kept going up and down over a number of days. So her brother Beppe asked me to take him to a wizard who lived at San Pancrazio, above the valley of the River Ambra. His real name was Barsimelli, but everybody called him Vulcano. We went by motorbike, so this must have happened after the war. We stopped on the way to ask a man where Vulcano lived and he pointed out the road: the wizard's house was at the top of a hill. We went on, and at the bottom of the hill we saw someone ploughing a field with a couple of oxen. When we got to the house we found Vulcano's daughter and said, 'We are looking for your father, could you call him?' She replied in a mysterious way, 'One doesn't call my father, he comes on his own accord.' 'But how can he know we've come?' 'He knows, he knows,' replied the girl.

We waited for a quarter of an hour and then the man who had been ploughing at the bottom of the hill appeared: of course he knew we had come, he had seen us pass! While we waited on the *aia* he went about his work without haste, unharnessing the oxen, putting them into the stable and giving them their food. Then he slowly walked up the stairs and went into the house. We were both intimidated by this gloomy-looking man (as, no doubt, was his intention), but finally Beppe plucked up courage, went up the stairs and knocked on the door. 'Come in!' said Vulcano. We went in and found him tranquilly tucking into some bread and ham. 'What do you want, young fellows?' he said brusquely. Almost stammering, Beppe explained about his sister's illness. Vulcano listened with a grave expression. Then he said, 'I'll look at once.' He got up and went into his bedroom. Goodness knows what he did there. I thought I could hear him opening and closing the shutters. Then he returned. 'Don't worry,' he said. 'It's nothing serious, she'll be better in a day or two.' And he went on eating his lunch.

Beppe gave the man ten lire and then we went away. Returning by the same road we met the man who had pointed out the way. He said, 'But what did you want from Vulcano?' We replied, 'Well, as you know, he's a wizard, so we went to ask his advice.' 'He's a wizard?' repeated the man laughing. 'I didn't know that! When we want to visit a wizard we go to a fellow called Gori Angelo who lives in Mercatale. What a funny thing,' he added in his Aretine dialect, 'you from there come here and we from here go there!' Now it was our turn to be astonished: Angelo was our field warden, we knew him well but we had no idea he was a wizard. But now we understood why peasants called him when their oxen were ill, evidently some people knew about his healing powers. I realized, also, the significance of something that had happened a couple of years earlier. One day I came across him and saw that his face and arms were covered with scratches. I thought that he had fallen into a bramble bush, but he explained that he had met the devil in the woods: 'He thought he could kill me with his claws, but I whacked him with my cane so hard that he ran away!'

And so we chatted about witches and wizards as we sat round the fire, and everyone had some experience to relate. We also talked about ghosts. These were the spirits of animals, or of dead people who came back to haunt us because they were damned. Some ghosts were associated with certain places: for example, the ghost of a calf could be seen near the brick kiln, while a sow used to haunt a piece of woodland near the stream. Round about Rendola you might see the ghost of a plucked turkey. After telling all these stories about ghosts many peasants were quite nervous about going out of the house after dark. At night the countryside was pitch black, there were no street lights even in the villages. When you are carrying a lantern, even someone who doesn't believe in ghosts during the day finds it easy to imagine them in the dark.

I remember a fellow called Morino who lived near Rendola, his house was where the riding stable is now. On Christmas Eve he went to Mass in the village and then walked home without a lantern, hoping not to meet the ghost of a plucked turkey on the way. He entered the house and groped his way to the mantelpiece to look for an oil lamp. Suddenly his face came into contact with a plucked turkey! The women of the house had prepared it for Christmas Day and had hung it up from the mantelpiece. Morino was so frightened that he let out a howl and jumped back, knocking over the table and the benches. There was such a tremendous din that the whole family woke up. His brother said: 'What the devil has happened, have the oxen escaped?' And someone else said: 'There's been an earthquake!' Everybody ran into the kitchen and found poor Morino stretched on the floor, white as a sheet. He had received such a shock that the next day he had a high temperature and had to spend Christmas in bed.

Sometimes, however, the peasants invented ghosts for a specific reason. For example, if they didn't want another family to take over their farm they would say it was haunted, they weren't quite sure by whom, but the place had an uncanny feel to it. So no one would want to live there.

Then a rumour went round that there was a werewolf in the woods. In fact, in the vicinity of Gretole you could hear howling. It made your hair stand on end. People were so afraid that they didn't go outside their houses at night. Except for Ghiere, one of the peasants of Gretole. Some of his grapes were missing, so he suspected a ruse. He said to his wife, 'This evening I'm going to have a look at this werewolf!' He took his gun and climbed up into a tree near his vineyard. After a long wait he heard that howling noise and something thrashing about in the woods, but he wasn't afraid: 'When that werewolf comes here I'll deal with him,' he said to himself. After a period of silence he could hear snip, snip, snip: somebody was cutting down the grapes. Quietly Ghiere climbed down from the tree and approached the vineyard. As he had suspected, he found his brother-in-law there stealing the grapes! He thwacked him well and truly with the butt of his gun and from that night onwards there was no more sign of the werewolf.

Nothing angered a peasant more than when somebody robbed him. He possessed so little, and if someone tried to steal what little he had it was a grave insult. People often told a tale about a peasant who kept his rabbits in a small shed in the middle of the fields. One day he realized that some of his rabbits were missing. So he went there at night-time and hid behind a bush to see if the thief was going to come back. Sure enough, after an hour or so he saw one of his neighbours approach. He had a tuft of grass in his hand and he put his arm into the window of the shed. Evidently, on previous occasions he had offered the rabbits some grass, and when one of them had approached the window he had grabbed it by the ears and pulled it out. But this time things went badly for our thief because the owner of the rabbits had shut them up in a cage and placed a fox trap right under the window. All of a sudden, bang! and the thief's fingers were caught in the trap. He couldn't even draw his hand out because the trap was too big to pass through the window. The peasant saw what had happened and had no pity. 'Aha,' he said, 'So this is the fox that has been stealing my rabbits. Ah well, he'll have the whole night to repent.' And he went off to bed. He freed the thief the following morning and I bet the fellow never tried to steal rabbits again.

Now and then, as we sat round the fire in the evening, a

144

cantastorie, a storyteller, would turn up. He was usually a peasant who had given up farming, evidently his talent could earn him more than farmwork did. He would sing traditional love stories for us, or he would sing about bandits, great heroes for us peasants, as they defied authority. Sometimes he would take as his theme something he had read about in the newspaper: I remember a song he sang about a girl who had been kidnapped and murdered in Livorno. When he had finished he would give us some sheets of paper where the words of the ballads were written. Naturally we gave him some coins and a glass or two of wine to help him to sing better. And if we liked his songs we would learn them too and sing them while we were working in the fields.

During the winter when the evenings were long, some of the peasants would get together to invent *zinganette*. These were little plays which had as their theme certain situations drawn from everyday life: when a future bride is preparing her trousseau, when a husband has to reveal to his wife that he has lost money gambling, when a son returns home after military service, and so on.

That was how we passed the evenings sitting round the fire. Nowadays people sit in silence in front of the television and hardly ever visit their neighbours. I wonder sometimes, are we better off?

In general we didn't travel about much, having worked all day long six days a week. Even Sunday was only partially a day of rest, because the oxen still had to be mucked out and fed, the pigs and sheep still had to be taken to the woods. In the morning the head of the family was obliged to go to Mass, if he didn't go his *padrone* wanted to know the reason why. The women went to Mass early so that they had time to prepare the Sunday lunch, the most important meal of the week. So after lunch, if there was no plan to visit relatives or go to a funeral, the head of the family liked to have a nap rather than venture out of the house.

But it was a different story where the young folk were concerned, they had plenty of energy to spare. They would often take a train and go and see the world. That usually meant Florence or Arezzo, about thirty and twenty miles away respectively. Or they would go to Siena to see the *Palio*, a twice-yearly horse race that was a great attraction, even if they didn't always arrive on time . . .

One day seven or eight young fellows decided to go and see the *Palio*. One of them, Beppe, was a carter's son, and was keen on seeing the racehorses, so much slimmer and more elegant than his father's nags. They had to take the train from Montevarchi to Sinalunga, travelling in a southerly direction, and then take another train for Siena, travelling westwards: the journey took more than three hours. During the first part of the journey Beppe stood with his head out of the window so that he could see better. It was a steam train, and when he arrived at Sinalunga his face was black with soot. A man was selling watermelon on the platform and as it was August and very hot they all bought a slice. No one can eat watermelon without getting the juice all over their faces, and you can imagine what Beppe looked like with his blackened face. A lady in the same compartment took pity on him, saying, 'Working in this heat must be hard for you charcoal-burners!'

At last the boys reached Siena. But the station is quite far from the Piazza del Campo and the street winds this way and that so it is easy to get lost. When they finally got to the square the race was over and the crowd had dispersed. So they contented themselves with wandering about the streets and getting lost again. When it began to get late they decided to take a bus home and made their way to the church of San Domenico, where all the buses stopped. But they discovered that the bus for Mercatale had just left. So they had to take another bus, the one that went to Montevarchi via Gaiole. As there were no seats left inside they climbed on to the luggage rack. In those days it was permitted to do this, I've often travelled that way myself. The journey went well as far as the village of Gaiole, but then the road wound up the hill through a dense forest and every now and then BRRRM! and they were hit by an overhanging branch. The blows were so violent that they had to cling on to the rack with all their might to avoid being swept off. By the time they got to Montevarchi they were covered from head to foot with cuts and bruises. And then they had to walk all the way to Mercatale, another four miles. When they got home their parents said, 'Look what happens when you go to the *Palio*! What a state you're in!' They thought the boys had been beaten up by the Sienese. The neighbourhoods that had lost the *Palio* often got overexcited and would vent their rage on anyone who happened to stand in their path.

A young friend of mine called Viticchi went to Siena too. He had just bought a second-hand bicycle and decided to travel round a bit. Everyone told him that the Sienese would play some trick on him because they would see at once that he came from the country. But he wanted to see the Piazza del Campo, even though the *Palio* wasn't being run that day. Finally he got there and sat on his bicycle looking round. The square is surrounded by beautiful buildings, but what drew Viticchi's attention was the enormous flock of pigeons hopping about. In the country a peasant might have ten or twelve pigeons, not more. Here there were hundreds of them! 'When I get home I'll tell them how many pigeons I've seen,' he said to himself. So he stuck out his forefinger and began to count them one by one. It wasn't an easy job because they kept fluttering about and, anyway, he wasn't used to counting more than the fingers on his hands. One of the Sienese saw him and realized at once that he was a country bumpkin. The fellow wore a uniform, but I don't think he was a policeman, he was probably a hotel porter. He went up to Viticchi and said, 'What are you doing, young man?' Viticchi replied, 'I'm counting the pigeons.' 'A-ha! Didn't you know it was forbidden to count them? I'll have to fine you!' 'Oh dear,' said Viticchi, crestfallen, 'I didn't know that! How much do I have to pay?' 'It depends. How many pigeons did you count?' 'A hundred.' 'Well then, the fine is one lira.' So poor Viticchi had to hand over a lira to the Sienese fellow.

When Viticchi got home he told us what had happened. 'They thought they could fool me in Siena,' he said, 'but I was more cunning than they were! When that policeman asked me how many pigeons I had counted I told him I had counted a hundred.' Then he lowered his voice, just in case they could hear him in Siena, thirty miles away. 'Don't tell anybody, but actually I had counted more than three hundred!'

On Saturday afternoons young people would often go dancing. The Red Cross had headquarters in many of the villages, at Mercatale, Levane and Moncioni. The members were all volunteers and when somebody fell ill they would push him to the hospital in a wheelbarrow. In order to augment their funds the organizations would often hire a band and hold a dance. The boys didn't go simply to dance, they went mainly to meet girls of their own age, otherwise they would see them only at Mass. It's not like nowadays when young people can meet each other in the street. In those days mothers would watch over their daughters like broody hens. In fact, when there was a dance, mothers would accompany their daughters to the hall and stay there until the dancing was over to make sure there was no hanky-panky.

A lot of young men went out even during the week to learn to play an instrument. Several villages had a band: there was one at Mercatale, for example, and also at Caposelvi, Levane and San Leolino. The aspiring musicians were keen to join a band because it was great fun to play with other people, and it was also a pretext for travelling around. I remember that the young men (no young women joined them) used to go to the Red Cross headquarters twice a week to take lessons from a maestro. He taught them to read music as well as play an instrument. There were at least fifty players in Mercatale alone, and the best ones were chosen to play in the band. I used to play the trumpet. On village feast days there was always a procession, and the band would follow playing religious marches. Then it would stop in the square and give a concert. We used to play marches and also arias from the operas of Verdi, Puccini and Rossini. But we didn't play anything light, the maestro wanted us to play only classical music. Everybody liked to listen, because before the war nobody had a radio and they thought listening to the local band was the height of entertainment.

After the war the bands of the smaller villages broke up one by one, so I went to play in the band of Montevarchi. I also played in the *fanfara dei bersaglieri* and once we went to northern Italy to play at the military cemetery of Redipuglia to commemorate 4 November, the day the First World War ended. But eventually I had to stop playing, because my teeth began to fall out and you can't play the trumpet with false teeth. But I can play the mouth organ pretty well. I learnt to play it by myself and I want to confess a curious thing: I keep the high notes on the left and the low notes on the right, because when I started there was nobody to tell me it should be the other way round. Actually, it doesn't make any difference, it's a question of habit. I usually play the songs I used to hear people singing in the fields, such as '*Il fazzolettino*', '*O campagnola bella*' and '*Rosamunda*'. In those days everybody used to sing while they worked. But who sings now? Tell me the truth, when did you last hear somebody sing? I know that since the war we have gained a good many things, but some we have also lost.

After the war the first cinema of Montevarchi opened. To see a film we had to go down to Montevarchi on foot, four miles there and four miles back. But we were used to walking and thought nothing of it. The very first film I saw was *Tarzan and the Apes*, in black and white. As a result my friends called me Tarzan, perhaps because I was very muscular. But the nickname didn't stick. After all I had no Jane to fall in love with me.

Then there were the village feast days, observed by everyone, as they broke up the monotony of everyday life. Every village, however small, had a church and every church had its patron saint. One day of the year was dedicated to that saint and that day was always a holiday. Each village had its *Compagnia di Fratelli*, its Company of Brothers. This was composed of peasants, workers, artisans and so on, all local people and all from the working classes. It was like a parliament in miniature. The Brothers would meet once a month in a room called the *stanza della compagnia*, the room of the company, which was next to the church, to discuss local problems with the priest and to organize feast days. They also took care of the needy, visited those who were ill and attended funerals. During the meetings the Brothers would sit on a bench that ran round the walls of the room, so that they were all equal. Most of the Brothers were men, but there were some women among them. It was considered an honour to belong to the Company. If someone wanted to join he would propose himself and the Brothers would vote by secret ballot: they each put a bean in a box if they were in favour, or a lupin seed if they were against. If there were more beans than lupin seeds the candidate would be admitted to the Company. It was a good way to vote because it didn't put people who couldn't read or write into difficulties.

Before the village feast day the Brothers would chose the *festaioli*, those who were responsible for the organization. There was always a religious procession and all the Brothers took part wearing white cloaks with hoods. One of them walked in front bearing the Cross, followed by two lines of Brothers, with the mace-bearer in the middle: he was the one who was in charge and he would walk up and down the procession to make sure nobody was neglecting his duty. Then came the priest and after him the Brother who was carrying the statue of Christ or the Virgin Mary or the Crucifix (it varied from village to village). Next to the priest and the Brother carrying the statue walked four Brothers holding the baldachin, and beside them walked the Brothers who had to carry the *lanternoni*, the ceremonial lanterns. It was hard work carrying these because you had to hold them up high. In fact the saying goes:

Gli stendardi e i lanternoni	Standards and lanterns
Toccano ai più coglioni!	Are the lot of the most foolish!

After the *lanternoni* came the band and finally the inhabitants of the village. But they didn't walk in silence – they chatted away, some of them even bartering and striking deals. Everybody took part, it was a wonderful experience because we felt that we all belonged to one big family.

A funny thing happened once during a procession at San Leolino. The feast day was on the first day of Lent and often the weather was bad. One year it snowed heavily two days before. The priest said to the Company, 'How can we have a procession with all this snow?' But the Brothers wanted to have a procession at all costs. The next day they harnessed oxen to carts and with the help of the other villagers they got down to work with their shovels and carried away all the snow that was in the middle of the street where the procession was to pass. So on the Sunday they were all full of excitement as they got together in front of the church and formed the procession. First went the Cross, and then the two lines of Brothers in their cloaks and hoods with the mace-bearer in the middle, then the priest. Suddenly the mace-bearer, a fellow called Gonnelli, stood still and raised his mace into the air. 'STOP, everybody!' he thundered. Everyone looked round, surprised. What did the fellow want? Gonnelli explained, 'My friends, we have forgotten Christ!' So they all had to go back to the church to fetch the statue.

Usually processions took place in the afternoon, so that in the morning there was time to go to Mass or a service. But everybody came home for lunch. Relations were invited along and a capon or a duck was killed to celebrate the occasion. Then, after the procession, everybody gathered in the square to hear the concert played by the band. Afterwards they stood and chatted, or bought some sweets at the stalls, or listened to a *cantastorie*. Sometimes the Brothers would organize games for the young men. I remember at Rendola in the middle of the square they put up a *palo della cuccagna*, a greasy pole: on top of it had been tied all sorts of prizes, bottles of wine, salamis and so on. The young men took turns to try to climb up the pole. Most of then slithered down again but sometimes one or two managed to get to the top, and everybody clapped. At Moncioni they had a contest which is still held today: the competitors have to roll along the road a flat wooden disc that resembles a sheep's cheese. Whoever rolls the disc furthest wins the prize.

The most important feast day for us was that of Mercatale. It fell on Palm Sunday so it was part of the Easter celebrations, and those started almost after Twelfth Night, with the beginning of Carnival. Young people loved Carnival because they could go dancing every Saturday and Sunday afternoon. Before the war people danced only during Carnival, so they had to take advantage of it while they could. The last Thursday of Carnival was called *Berlingaccio* and it was the tradition to eat meat on that day:

Berlingaccio,	Berlingaccio,
Chi non ha ciccia mangia il gatto.	He who has no meat can eat the cat.

It was also called *la festa dei becchi*, the cuckolds' feast day, but I don't know why. It seems to me that if you're a cuckold you'd prefer to keep the fact under your hat.

The following Tuesday was the last day of Carnival and we would go dancing *in maschera*, disguised: but we only put on a mask, a piece of material with holes for eyes and mouth. In the dance hall there was always someone who played the role of Death, because Carnival died on that day. Four members of the company would carry him in on a bier and he had to lie there motionless until midnight. At that hour the priest would go to the church to ring the bells and everybody had to go home, including

Death. Now Lent had begun and it was no longer permitted to have a good time.

On one occasion Death didn't go home. There was a party at Moncioni in the house of a fellow called Soldani. Four masked men brought Death in as usual and then took part in the festivities. At midnight the church bells rang and people began to go home. Someone said to Death, 'Come on, get up, the party's over.' But Death didn't get up because he really was dead. Poor Soldani got into a lot of trouble about the murder, although he had nothing to do with it. This is why it is now forbidden to go around in a mask – evidently it gave people the opportunity to commit murder without being recognized.

The first Wednesday of Lent was Ash Wednesday. People went to church and the priest put a pinch of ashes on their heads to signify penitence. Then, until Easter, there were sermons every Sunday. They were in Italian so at least one could understand, not like the prayers which were in Latin. The preacher was usually one of the monks from the Capuchin monastery near Montevarchi. I often went, because when I came out of the church I could meet up with my friends, and there was a chance to chat up the girls as well. During Lent it was forbidden to eat meat, we could only eat eggs and fish. It was said that this rule was brought in by St Peter because he was a fisherman and wanted to sell more of his catch. It was during this period that young people would *fare al verde*, show something green: they would keep a sprig of boxwood in their pockets and would pull it out every time someone challenged them with the words: 'Show something green!' If they didn't have a sprig they would have to pay a forfeit.

On Palm Sunday, Mercatale's feast day, the peasants would take an olive branch to church to have it blessed, and then they would attach sprigs of it all over the place, inside and outside the house, in the stable, even out in the fields, to ward off the evil eye. The church was adorned with dark orange velvet drapes and Mass was celebrated three times a day. At eleven o'clock three monks would enact the Passion: one told the story, one took the part of Christ and the other played the roles of Judas, Pilate and Caiaphas, the Jewish high priest. Unfortunately they sang in Latin, so nobody understood very much of it. Then we went home for lunch. In the afternoon there was a procession and the band took part in it. I would go and play too. Then as usual the band would hold a concert in the square in front of the villagers. Playing makes you thirsty, so after the concert the Brothers would organize refreshments outside the church: they would offer us holy wine and *brigadini*, a kind of little biscuit.

But that wasn't the end of the celebrations, because the next day was the fair where oxen were bought and sold. The peasants who had an animal to sell would wash it until it was as white as snow. You could tell which ox had been bought by the butcher because it was decorated with red ribbons, on its muzzle, round the neck and at the end of its tail. And even if you had nothing to sell you would go to the fair all the same because it was a jolly occasion and you wanted to meet up with all your relations who had gone there too. The streets swarmed with people, there were stalls all over the place and likely as not a *cantastorie* was performing and selling his song sheets.

In the afternoon there was the bicycle race, they still hold it – it's become a tradition. Nobody knows when it started, perhaps when bicycles were invented. The cyclists went round the same route several times and every time they passed through Mercatale I was the one who had to warn the public: I stood beside the bridge over the Tricesimo, and when I saw the cyclists appear at the top of the village I would play some notes on my trumpet, 'da da da daaa!' and everybody would get out of the way.

People came from all over the Arno valley to see the fair and watch the bicycle race. Once two poets came on their bicycles, one from Levane and the other from beyond the Arno. They met outside the *bottega* and evidently they knew each other, because one gave the other an *ottava rima*, the traditional verse used by local poets. These two poets couldn't read or write but they could improvise poetry, it was a gift of nature. The other poet replied with an *ottava rima*, and then began to push his bicycle up the hill because he wanted to go home. When he was almost at the top and was about to bicycle away the other poet shouted out another *ottava rima*, so the bicyclist was compelled to return. So it went on all afternoon, because each one wanted to be the last to reply. At some point I went home to have supper, and when I came back they were still at it, and by this time a crowd had formed round them to see who would win the contest. I don't know who was the victor, because finally I had to go home to sleep. I suppose they called a truce.

At that time there were a lot of poets around and they often held contests on feast days to entertain the crowd. Someone gave them a theme and they would invent *ottava rima* after *ottava rima* for hours on end. Some of these *contrasti* were famous, but I know of only one that was written down, a quarrel between a Florentine citizen and a peasant who happened to meet at a hostelry. I know it off by heart as I've sung it myself on feast days in the square of Rendola. The two exchange insults for several verses and then finally the peasant says:

Quei prosciutti, quei salami e quelle spalle	Those hams, salamis and shoulders
Fra noi villani mangeremo insieme,	We peasants will eat together,
Tacchi, piccioni, galletti e pollastre	Turkeys, pigeons, cockerels and pullets,
E tu, grullarello, a Firenze mangerai . . . le lastre!	While you, blockhead, in Florence You'll eat . . . paving stones!

Naturally I sing the part of the peasant, and when I get to these last lines I shout them out so loud they can almost hear me in Montevarchi.

Before Easter the priest went round blessing the houses. The housewives cleaned the house from top to bottom, they even cleaned behind the cupboards. Perhaps they were afraid that the priest might look there. The men cleaned the stable and the wine cellar, they removed the cobwebs and swept behind the barrels. It was simply a good excuse to do a general clean-up. However, people believed that if you didn't get your house blessed before Easter some evil might befall the family. By way of thanking the priest we would give him some eggs. Goodness knows how many omelettes he made over that period.

Now Good Friday was approaching and the tension was building. We knew that something terrible was going to happen, the death of Jesus. On the Monday and the Tuesday before, the Brothers would hold a vigil: in the church Christ on his crucifix would be covered up and the Brothers would take turns to watch over Him so that He would never remain alone. Then on the Thursday the women would decorate the altar with flowers. It was called 'preparing the Holy Sepulchure', the place where Jesus was buried. The women would vie with each other to see who could bring the most beautiful flowers. In the afternoon we would *visitare le chiese*, visit the churches. We were supposed to visit seven, but as there were only five in the area, those at Mercatale, Rendola, Caposelvi, La Torre and Galatrona, we visited two of them twice: we would go in, go out and then go in again. We young fellows strolled round in a group, the girls formed another group, and of course we found some way to meet up. We used to take with us a *bastone fiorito*, a flowering stick: we cut off a branch of dogwood and with a knife removed parts of the bark in a spiral pattern. After visiting the churches we went to the church of Mercatale, where the priest would be waiting for us. He would tell us the story of Christ on the cross, and when he reached the moment that Christ died and there was an earthquake we made as much noise as possible, banging our sticks against the floor and the benches. It was the only time that the priest actually encouraged us to make a noise in church, so we took advantage of the occasion.

Then we had to calm down because there was a sermon. At eleven o'clock in the evening the church bells were rung and then they were tied up until Saturday morning. Normally they were rung at midday and at seven o'clock, and this was very useful because very few people had watches. For a couple of days we had to tell the time by the sun, but that was impossible when it was cloudy. To replace the bells the priest used to stand outside the church and make a noise with a rattle, but you could only hear that in the village, not out in the fields.

The next day was Good Friday and there was a procession at night. It was a wonderful spectacle with all the lanterns, torches and candles, everyone bringing what they could. We took the statue of Christ out of the church and followed a long route round the countryside, with all the Brothers in their white cloaks and hoods, the band playing funeral marches and the inhabitants of the villages bringing up the rear. First we went through the village of La Torre and then we went down to the stream. It was often difficult to ford it without getting our feet wet, so, seeking to curry favour with the local people, the Fascists built a bridge there. But they made it too narrow and with parapets that were too high, so that when we passed over it with the statue of Christ we had to lift it up into the air. You should have heard the swearing that went on. Then we climbed the hill on the other side and passed by the *Crocifisso*, that is to say, the turning for Caposelvi, and then back to Mercatale.

On the Saturday afternoon or early on the Sunday morning we had to make our confessions before going to Mass and here a problem arose. If we went to our parish priest he would ask us when was the last time we had confessed and we were ashamed to say we hadn't confessed for a year, not since the previous Easter. So we went to confess ourselves at the Capuchin monastery down near Montevarchi. Lots of people went there, having found themselves in the same situation. It was clear that in a whole year we had all committed quite a number of sins, even if it was simply a matter of swearing, which all Tuscans have a habit of doing. So the priest would give us a quantity of penances, like a hundred Ave Marias, a hundred Paternosters. It was ridiculous: how could we possibly carry out these penances before going to Mass? Luckily the monks had already foreseen this difficulty, because when we came out of the monastery we found two monks sitting outside who, for a consideration, would say the prayers for us.

On Easter Sunday everybody went to Mass, even those who weren't really believers. Christ was uncovered because he had by now risen again and the priest would ring the bells to proclaim the miracle. Then we all went home and had a big lunch: we usually ate stewed lamb with spinach. At Mercatale the following day was also a holiday, because it was the feast day of the Redeemer, the patron of the village. So we made another procession, this time with the Christ which was in the room beside the church where the Brothers held their meetings. There is an identical crucifix in the church of San Lorenzo in Montevarchi. The story goes that a carpenter saw a service tree and announced, 'I'm going to carve a crucifix out of this tree!' He told his friends to shut him up inside his workshop and to feed him by means of a trapdoor. Days later they unlocked the door of the workshop and found not one crucifix but two; the carpenter, however, had vanished. People said that a miracle had occurred, but I think that the fellow had a shrewish wife and that he had taken the opportunity to run away from home.

Easter was the most important feast day of the year, but there were many other, minor ones. They often fell on a Sunday, when we didn't work anyway, but we still felt those Sundays were different from the others. Before Easter came St Joseph's Day, 19 March, when it was the custom to make *frittelle*, rice fritters. We made them only on that day, as they used up too much olive oil to make them more often. That way we appreciated them all the more. After Easter came Ascension Day. I don't know what it represented but it was one of my favourite feast days because we always went for a picnic. The inhabitants of Mercatale used to go up to a field under the Tower of Galatrona and have a picnic all together, but at Casa del Bosco we used to invite our relations and eat out in the fields. This was usually the moment to start eating the *finocchiona*, the salami with fennel seeds in it. Nobody ever worked that day, the saying goes: '*Non vanno nemmeno gli uccelli al nido*' – 'The birds don't even fly to their nests.'

On Corpus Domini we used to scatter petals on the road, the petals of wild roses, daisies and broom, whatever we could lay our hands on. Then we had a procession with the statue of Christ, as it was his feast day. At the end of June there was the feast day of St Peter and St Paul. Perhaps they weren't very important so they had to share a day. The evening before we would light a bonfire in the fields. All the peasants tried to outdo one other and make the biggest bonfire and it was a beautiful sight with all the fireflies dancing around. But usually the peasants didn't take a day off then because the harvest was approaching and there was too much to do. There weren't any feast days during the rest of the summer. Maybe the good Lord didn't consider that we needed any because we used to have a nap during the middle of the day. The next holiday was All Saints' Day, on 1 November. On that day we used to take flowers to our loved ones in the cemetery, people still do it. We'd take roses, carnations, sweet william, mallow: whatever we had in the garden, but nobody had much because of the shortage of water. After that we would eat roast chestnuts, according to the tradition.

Then there was Christmas Day. We didn't eat meat the day before – we never did on the day preceding a feast day. As the proverb tells us:

Chi guasta la vigilia di Natale	He who spoils Christmas Eve
Corpo di becco e anima di cane!	Has a goat's body and a dog's soul!

Then at midnight we went to Mass and sang the carol '*Tu scendi dalle stelle*', 'You descend from the starry sky'. The next day it was the custom to kill a capon and have a good feast. Then came New Year's Day, but we didn't celebrate it as much as people do now. It was a holiday and we went to Mass, that's all. We had a good lunch and in the evening we visited our neighbours. The next feast day was Epiphany, the children's holiday. We used to explain to the small children that the *Befana* was a sort of good witch who used to go round with a little donkey giving presents. Before going to sleep the children had to put their shoes out at the bottom of the bed. In the middle of the night she would come down the chimney and fill the shoes of the good children with fruit and sweets, but the naughty children would get only lumps of coal. So in the evening we helped the children prepare on the hearth a little pile of firewood for the *Befana* so that she could warm herself, and a bundle of hay for her donkey. Nowadays children know more about Father Christmas than the *Befana*, but in those days we hadn't even heard of him and it seems sad to me that we are losing a tradition that is well and truly Italian.

After Epiphany the Carnival period started and so we were back to the beginning. The year was like a great wheel, turning all the time. We peasants worked hard, but there was always a feast day approaching and we worked all the more willingly in anticipation of it. There are still some feast days left, but people appreciate them less because they have more free time now. It is better like this, but people of my generation miss the feast days of the past because we valued them more.

CHAPTER 7

After the War

I can recall the events of my life quite clearly, but I can't always remember when they happened. We were too busy with the farm work to think about dates and one year would slip into the next. But one thing is certain: the war constituted a watershed between the years that preceded it and those that followed. Almost all the changes in my life belong to the years after the war, not before it. In spite of all the rhetoric, Mussolini did little to improve our lives and it was hard not to mock what little he did.

One thing that Mussolini did was to give orders to the *padroni* to build lavatories for us. These usually consisted of little rooms stuck on to the outer wall of our houses. No gleaming ceramic bowl for us, however! Only a plank of wood with a hole in it. Whatever you put into it passed down a pipe made of earthenware segments leading to the *pozza nera*, the 'black well' where the liquid manure from the stables also accumulated. You had to keep a wooden cover over the hole, otherwise the stench from below would fill the house. It was a primitive system, but at least we no longer had to go out of the house. This, actually, had been no problem for us because the woods were just behind the house. But imagine what it was like for anyone who lived in the square of Mercatale: he or she would have to walk quite far to find a quiet spot to squat in, and there was always the fear that someone would find you with your underpants down. Thank you, Mussolini! But if you had told our *padroni* to bring piped water to our

161

houses, then we could have had flushing lavatories, such as no doubt you had in your house!

Mussolini also told the *padroni* to build proper manure pits. Before we used to put the manure into a hole in the ground, but it fermented much better in a structure made of bricks with a pit in the centre where the liquid could collect. Once again, thank you, Mussolini! You were rightly concerned about hygiene; but if you had also thought of giving us wood stoves so that we could have heated our cold, damp houses, we would have been much more grateful. You could have given the peasants insurance and a pension too, like the factory workers. No, we were third-class citizens, we had to be content with lavatories and manure pits.

During the Fascist regime the Socialist and Communist parties were suppressed and went underground. I'm talking about what happened in the towns: in the country we hardly knew they existed. Most of the peasants belonged to the Fascist Party, but only because they were more or less forced to, not because they believed in it. If the Fascists discovered that you were a member of one of the left-wing parties they would beat you up, they might even kill you. I heard about a fellow from Montegonzi who had a membership card for the Socialist Party and he walled it up in a hole in the wall of his well, saying:

Qui ti muro, qui ti lascio,	Here I wall you up, here I leave you,
Vent'anni durerà il Fascio.	The Fascist regime will last for twenty years.

And that's what happened.

After the fall of Fascism, Communism and Socialism could come out into the open again and many of the peasants joined one or other of the two parties. They were full of enthusiasm because they felt that at last there was someone who took an interest in their problems. Previously, they had had the impression that they were the victims of a plot: the *padrone* would instruct them to go to Mass and do what the priest told them, while the priest instructed them to work hard and do what the *padrone* told them. There was no way out! But now things were different and although nothing much changed immediately after the war because the country was on its knees, at least we felt that improvements were on their way.

The peasants didn't really know the difference between the Socialist or Communist parties – perhaps they were more similar in those days. The propagandists of the two parties would go round the countryside to enrol new members, and if a Socialist came to your house you would join his party, while if a Communist came you would join his. I know a family who lived on the two floors of the same house: on the ground floor a Socialist persuaded those he could find to join the Socialist Party, while a Communist went up to the first floor, with the result that the rest of the family joined the Communist Party. There must have been lively discussions in that family for years afterwards!

Naturally the *padroni* weren't too happy about the situation and began to feel afraid. The priest was on their side and preached to the peasants that they must join the Christian Democrat Party. In fact, the priest up at Moncioni must have been particularly convincing because a lot of the peasants there became Christian Democrats. But in Mercatale and Rendola we didn't pay heed to the priest and most of us joined the Communist Party. I became a Communist in 1946 when I was nineteen years old and, I am proud to say, I still am a Communist. At Mercatale the party was very active and during the meetings our leaders explained to us how to vote for the *Assemblea Costituente*, the assembly elected to draw up a new constitution after the fall of the Fascist regime, and also for the referendum, where the Italian people would be asked to choose between the monarchy and a republic. Under the Fascist regime we had never had a chance to vote and we needed some advice, particularly those among us who could barely read and write. They must have explained to us well, because a lot of Communists and Socialists were elected to the Assembly: between them they numbered more than the Christian Democrats. As for the referendum, the monarchy was thrown out because many Italians didn't think it had any purpose. If you have a democratic republic the citizens can always vote against a government they don't like and choose another one; while if you have a royal family like ours which isn't much good you are saddled with it all the same, there's no way of changing it.

At that time I was still working from dawn to dusk in the fields, so attending meetings was a *sacrificio*, but I still went because I realized that at last improvements were going to be made in our living conditions. We all felt that our leaders were really on our side, not just pretending to be so like other politicians. We also went to the trade union meetings: the CGIL (the General Italian Confederation of Workers) had already been founded and it included Federterra, the union that concerned itself with the problems of the peasants. During these meetings the peasants listened to the speakers but didn't open their mouths because they were too shy. The leader of the CGIL was a man called Di Vittorio: he had only completed primary school so he understood why we didn't dare to speak. He once went to a meeting and asked a member of the audience why nobody made any contribution to the discussion. The man replied, 'Well, you see, we have had very little schooling and we are afraid we might say something stupid.' 'I too have had very little schooling,' replied Di Vittorio, 'but I have learnt this: when a worker says five words, at least three of them are right.' I read this in the Communist paper *Unità* and it consoled me, because I was shy too and didn't open my mouth much during meetings. But it was important to participate all the same. Not only in the meetings, in the demonstrations as well: the more of us the better.

It was during this period that a *carabiniere* came to check my movements almost every week. To tell the truth, my movements were from one field to another, ploughing, sowing, digging and pruning, whatever job I had to do at the time. What on earth did he think I was doing, plotting a revolution, making bombs? Poor fellow, he had to bicycle all the way up from Mercatale. He always invented an excuse: for example, he would say that some poultry had been stolen in the area and asked whether any of my hens were missing. But he didn't fool me, I knew perfectly well why he had come. He was only doing his duty, so I didn't mind.

At that time we attended demonstrations partly because we were fighting for the right to have piped water and electricity brought to our houses, but above all because we wanted the produce of the land to be shared out more fairly. We wanted to keep back sixty per cent of the produce, not fifty per cent, which was all we were entitled to by the existing laws (actually, we would like to have abolished the sharecropping system altogether, but our leaders said that it was better not to be in too much of a hurry and to make reforms one at a time). In the end the government said that we could have fifty-three per cent, and we had to be content with that for the time being. I think it was in the fifties that we also demonstrated against Pacciardi, the Minister of Defence. Things were very tense because many people thought that the Russian Communists were preparing to take over the world and that the Italian Communists would give them a hand. They were also afraid that the city of Trieste would be handed over to Tito's Communists, but in fact it was given back to Italy. At any rate, this fellow Pacciardi sent a letter to everyone who had taken part in the war, telling them to prepare for call-up. These preliminary letters were usually sent to those who had to do military service: later a postcard would come telling them to go to the nearest barracks for a medical examination. So those who had already served in the war were indignant. 'What's all this about?' they said angrily. 'We have just finished one war and you're asking us to fight in another?' So we demonstrated about that too. The *bandiere della pace*, the flags of peace, began to appear all over the place: they were made of coloured cloth and the *contadini* put them on the top of the strawstacks while they were threshing the grain (those letters had began to arrive during the summer).

It was the time of year that all the peasants got together to help each other with the threshing, and we wanted to make a protest also about something else: during that busy time we were expected to work from half-past three in the morning until sunset, and all we were asking for was a pause in the middle of the day. The *padroni* wanted us to work without a break (I would like to have seen them work in our place!), and not only them, but also the owners of the threshing machines. So they sent the *carabinieri* and they ordered us to take the flags down. Of couse, as soon as they left we put the flags up again. At the *fattoria* of Petrolo at Galatrona the *padrone* sent the *carabinieri* to take down the flags and immediately other flags appeared, tied to the oak trees on the estate.

I made my protest against Pacciardi too. I was now the party treasurer at Mercatale and sometimes I used to write the *giornale murale*, a sort of newspaper written on a noticeboard attached to the wall. In Montevarchi you can still see such newspapers, written by members of the various parties. I was an enthusiastic member of the party, and, like many others, had helped to build the *Casa del Popolo*, the party headquarters and social centre. Of course, we were all volunteers and we worked in our free time, often at night. I was now more sure of myself, as the party had given me confidence. One day I asked a carpenter friend of mine to prepare me a tin of glue mixed with cinnabar, a mineral which is used to tint earthenware red. Then one night I carried a ladder into the square, climbed up it and wrote on the wall: '*Pacciardi, sei il nemico della gioventù*', 'You are the enemy of young people!' You can still see the letters above the shop where they sell washing machines. People have often tried to paint the letters out, but they always appear again. Obviously it is impossible to conceal the truth.

At about that time something happened at the *fattoria* of Rendola which was a serious business, but it also had its comic side. One of the peasants present told me about it. The *maestro di casa*, the man who represented the owner, was an elderly marquis. One day he had entered the administrative office with a newspaper in his hand, saying that the Prefect had declared that it was illegal to put up the flags of peace. Somebody immediately replied: 'The *Nazione* is the newspaper of the *padroni*, try reading the *Unità* and you'll get a different opinion!' By now the peasants bore the Marquis little respect. There were more than thirty peasants on the estate and they wanted to receive better treatment. They made an appointment with the Marquis and the bailiff and on the established day they all went along to the office. A number of women went along too. They argued and argued but made no headway, it was clear that the Marquis was not prepared to budge an inch. In the end the peasants declared that the Marquis and his bailiff could not leave the office until they had signed the agreement. Some of them thumped the table so hard that they upset the inkwell and the ink ran all over the place. At nightfall the *carabinieri* turned up and they sent everybody home.

The next day all the peasants who had taken part in the confrontation were summoned to the *carabinieri* headquarters and accused of 'violation of private property and sequestration of persons'. The secretary of our trade union, Federterra, was present too to give them moral support. One of the peasant's wives, a lady called Natalina Vasai, saved the situation. 'Listen, Mr Commissar, the electric wires pass right across our *podere*, but the *padrone* has always refused to bring electricity to our house. When my daughter comes back from school she has to take the pigs into the wood, so when the time comes for her to do her homework it is already dark. But Mr Commissar, could *you* study with a light like this?' Then she pulled an olive-oil lamp out of her bag and waved it about.

The Commissar was not a bad man, he began to laugh heartily and then he sent everybody home. But the law has to take its course, and after a while a trial was held at Arezzo. The secretary of Federterra hired a coach to take the accused there, all forty-nine of them! The interrogations went on all day, and you can imagine how frightened those peasants were. None of them had been inside a lawcourt before. The judge wanted to find out who had been the ringleader behind what amounted to a rebellion. But he didn't manage to incriminate anybody. In the end he decided that the episode had happened spontaneously and absolved them all.

My own family never had such a dramatic confrontation with our *padrone*; yet after the war our relationship began to change, at first almost imperceptibly, and then more and more. Groppa Secca had had such a shock when some Germans had forced him to give them the keys of his cellar that he became a little less tyrannical. It was not that he repented of the way he had treated us, but that he realized for the first time that he was vulnerable. One should add that he was also growing old – he was already in his seventies at the end of the war. He began to leave more and more decisions to his bailiff and walked round his property less, though he never completely stopped doing so until his last days. This bailiff was called Pietro like me and perhaps this was the reason that we got on well. He had a difficult role to play because he realized that our requests were reasonable, and yet he still had to stay in the good graces of his master.

This conflict became clear when piped water was finally brought to Casa del Bosco. There had always been a shortage of water at Casino del Monte and Casa del Bosco. One day my brother Azeglio said to the bailiff, 'There's a small spring in the woods on the other side of the valley, higher than these two houses: the water could be brought here without using a pump.' So the bailiff called a technician from Montevarchi. He brought with him an instrument, and with this he could see that the water would certainly come on its own accord as far as Casino del Monte, and therefore without doubt as far as our own house which was lower down. So Groppa Secca paid for the materials (that must have made him suffer!) and the peasants of the two houses put in the labour. Lisca, the peasant at Le Muricce, didn't have any water either, and he made a pact with the foreman who was in charge: the technician had said that the water would reach the landing halfway up the stairs of Casino del Monte, but Lisca persuaded the builder to place the tank some yards below the house. Then he asked the bailiff if he could have the overflow. It's said that Lisca gave the builder a demijohn of wine to help him make the decision ... Nowadays there are *bustarelle*, envelopes containing money. Then there were demijohns. Isn't it the same thing? But everybody behaved that way; at times I've done so myself. In Lisca's position I would probably have done exactly the same. Anyway, Lisca took the overflow and so the peasant at Casino del Monte had less water. Then we laid down pipes as far as our own house. The water was brought to a tap just outside our kitchen, so I said to Pietro, 'Let's make a hole in the wall, so that we can bring the water to a tap over the sink.' But Pietro frowned and said, 'No, let's wait. Later, perhaps . . .' He knew Groppa Secca well: that miserable old man would have thought that having piped water as far as the kitchen sink was too much of a luxury for a simple peasant. But I was no longer afraid of Groppa Secca, so I made the hole there and then and brought the water to a tap over the sink. Some days later Groppa Secca saw it but he made no comment. That was another sign that times had changed.

We are now so used to having piped water in our houses that it doesn't seem important, but then it was a real luxury. We no longer had to lug water all the way up from the spring. Now we had plenty of water to drink and to cook with. We could even wash ourselves more often, even though we didn't have a bathroom. There was enough for the oxen and we could water the vegetable garden: before we had had to use water from the pond, but that would almost dry up during the summer when it was most needed and what was left had hardly been enough for the animals.

It was about at this time that electricity was brought to Casa del Bosco. Previously it had only reached Le Muricce, but now Pietro had it brought to our house, three hundred yards further up. The transformer room was down at the *Crocifisso* near Mercatale, a long distance away, so the current was very weak by the time it reached our house. We could barely read by it, but as we were used to paraffin lamps, electricity seemed miraculous to us. It even powered the chaff-cutter, though we had to give it a push now and then to make it go round.

For us peasants electricity was a mysterious thing and we were slightly apprehensive of it: even changing a light bulb put us into a state of agitation. We didn't really understand how it worked, I don't think I do even now. Certainly our friend Quirino who ate the plate of earthworms didn't understand it. They had brought electricity to his house too, and after a while a couple of light bulbs blew, so he went to the *bottega* to buy some more. He was rather tightfisted, and when he heard how much they cost he asked: 'But haven't you got any second-hand ones?' 'Certainly!' said the shopkeeper, and he produced a cardboard box full of the bulbs that the peasants had given him when they bought new ones. 'You can take them all, and as you are a friend I will sell them to you at a special price!' Believing that he had made a bargain, Quirino paid for the boxful of bulbs and then carried it home. The following day he came back, looking very upset. 'Do you remember those second-hand light bulbs you sold me yesterday? Well, I've tried them all and not a single one works!'

This episode reminds me of the day they brought electricity to San Leolino. In the 1920s there was already electricity at Bucine down in the valley, and one day the local authorities decided to extend the line as far as San Leolino. The villagers were very happy when they heard the news and asked themselves which route the electricity would take. They made all sorts of guesses, but the most expert among them declared it would come up from Casariccio, the house at the bridge at the bottom of the hill, because that was where the electricity poles ended.

So the necessary work was done and one Sunday at Mass the priest announced that the following Sunday the light would come. The villagers decided to do something to celebrate this momentous event, and they agreed to bring out the village band to 'meet the light'. After Mass on the following Sunday the members of the band assembled in the square and set off down the hill playing a march with all the villagers behind them. When they got to Casariccio they placed themselves in the middle of the road and played another march. After pausing for a chat they played yet another march and so it went on all morning. And still the light didn't arrive. 'When's this blessed light going to come?' they asked themselves and started to play again.

Then at about midday, when they were all beginning to get hungry, a woman shouted down from the village on top of the hill, 'The light's arrived! The light's arrived!'

The members of the band and all the others who had followed them down to Casariccio looked at each other with amazement. '*Madonna buona*! We've been waiting here all morning and we didn't see the light come! Whichever road did it take?'

The inhabitants of San Leolino are embarrassed about this story and say that it isn't true. But I know this is what really happened because I was told about it by Gonnelli, the peasant who lived at Casariccio. Everyone in the Arno valley knows the story and has had a good laugh about it.

During the years that followed the war my mother still had to do the cooking over the open fire. This involved a lot of work, because we had to prepare the wood and keep the fire going even during the summer. She had to bend over as she worked, and in the summer it was uncomfortably hot. It wasn't until the fifties that we were able to buy a *cucina economica*, a wood stove. This could be used for cooking, but it would also heat the room, and much more efficiently than the open fire on the hearth, where most of the heat went up the chimney. It also used up less wood. A lot of houses in the country still have these stoves. Of course, before the war all the *padroni* had one – I remember seeing one in Groppa Secca's kitchen – but now the peasants could have one too, something that was unthinkable before the war. It seemed to us such a luxury. We no longer had to jostle for a place near the fire, the whole kitchen was warm now. It didn't matter to us that our bedrooms were still cold, as we were already warm ourselves when we went to bed, and anyway we had the priest to take the chill off the sheets. Later on we also bought a small gas stove. This was also a useful invention because we could use it in the summer when the wood stove was no longer burning.

In the years after the war I was always busy. During the day I worked on the farm with Azeglio and Edoardo, then I would go out almost every evening: either to a meeting organized by the Communist Party, or I had to practise with the band. Sometimes I would go dancing or visit my neighbours. I had been very shy as a child, but now I began to come out of my shell, and anyway, life offered young people more amusements than before: we had a little more money at our disposal too and there was a sense of freedom in the air now that the Fascists were no longer in power. I also think that belonging to the Communist Party gave us more courage and initiative. It taught us to be proud and not ashamed that we were peasants, so we were no longer resigned to our fate and prepared to be bossed about. The *padroni* had become less domineering: they didn't ask us any more for all those extra little gifts, like the capons Boccio took to Florence, and Groppa Secca kept quiet if we didn't go to Mass. To tell the truth, I still went. It was the custom. At one time I was even a member of the Company of Brothers at Mercatale. It is true that I was a Communist, but the Church had always been part of my life, and even though I wasn't particularly religious, I still liked to participate in all the rites and festivities the Church provided.

Then the lightning struck: in 1950 Pope Plus XII excommunicated all the Communists. This meant that we could no longer attend Mass or belong to the Company. Don Omero, the priest of

Mercatale, made a dramatic stand: he told the Brothers that they had to renounce their membership of the Communist Party before the altar. 'I'm now going into the sacristy,' he said, 'and when I come back in three minutes' time you must all take this oath.' But when he returned the Brothers had all vanished! They took with them the key of the Company's meeting place, so for the next

Pietro at the age of 29.

procession Don Omero had to borrow all the ceremonial lanterns and banners from a neighbouring parish. He also had no Brothers left to organize and take part in the procession. Other priests sent the Brothers forms which they had to fill in and declare that they didn't belong to the Communist or Socialist Parties. Just think of it, Communists used to call each other 'comrade' in the same way as the Brothers did, and now the Church wanted to throw them out! Many Brothers were compelled to leave the Companies because they didn't want to fill in these forms. As a result most of the companies were dissolved. When the Church backtracked and began to accept anyone, even Communists, people were too angry and offended to join the Companies again.

In my opinion the Pope made a great mistake when he excommunicated the Communists. I know that our party was opposed to religion of every kind, but most people were happy to remain Catholics in spite of the fact that they were Communists. We didn't feel there was any contradiction. We sang the Red Flag, but still had our children baptized. What was wrong with that? With that excommunication the Pope alienated a lot of people from the Church and many of them never returned even when the Church's attitude became more relaxed.

However, I wasn't all that worried. I must say it was a relief not to have to go to the Cappuccini monastery any more to confess all the sins I had committed in the previous year (mostly swearing). My days were so busy, I had no time to think about religion.

It was at that time that I had bought my first motorized vehicle: an English motorbike. After the war the Allies departed, leaving behind a large number of motorbikes, cars and trucks. It's true that most of them were rather ramshackle by now, but they were much prized by the Italians, most of whom possessed no means of transport at all other than a bicycle. All those vehicles were taken to big depots, where you could buy them cheaply. I bought my motorbike from Tono, a smith who had come to live at Le

Muricce, so I wasn't its first Italian owner. Once I'd bought it I naturally wanted to show it off to everybody, so one evening two friends, climbed on behind me and off we went towards Levane. Neither the brakes nor the headlight worked very well, and when we came down the steep hill on the other side of Caposelvi we collided with a flock of sheep. We knocked about ten of them over before we were able to stop, and the sheepdog might have torn us to pieces if we hadn't given him a bit of a bump too. That quietened him down! We got a few bruises and grazed our legs a bit, that's all, we were lucky to escape so lightly.

When the motorbike didn't work any more I bought a Lambretta, and I used that during the last years I worked as a peasant. I had got my driving licence in 1949 and sometimes Tono would ask me to drive people from one place to another. For example, I would often take the television technicians up to the transmitter at Monteluco. I also learnt to drive a tractor, and sometimes people would hire my services. But for working my own land oxen had to do, in Groppa Secca's opinion.

Meanwhile Tono had become my father-in-law. When he moved with his family to Le Muricce I made the acquaintance of his daughter, Franca. We went dancing together and soon we fell in love. After an engagement of three or four years we decided to get married. First, however, I took Franca to the Villino to present her to Groppa Secca, as was the custom. To show his approval he had our future bedroom at Casa del Bosco whitewashed. We got married at the Church of Mercatale in 1956 (by this time Communists were permitted to have a religious ceremony). For our honeymoon we went to Vada, near Follonica. It was the first time either of us had seen the sea. We didn't have a bathe, though, as neither knew how to swim, and we couldn't have learnt in the stream near the house as the water only came up to our ankles.

We spent the first eight years of our marriage at Casa del Bosco and there our two sons were born, Giorgio and Sergio. Then Groppa Secca died and his heirs took possession of the property.

A year later I obtained permission to move to a farmhouse near Mercatale. The place had its disadvantages: the house itself was very cold, because it stood in the path of a current of air coming

Pietro and Franca on their wedding day.

up from the valley, and there was very little water in the summer as the well dried up regularly in times of drought. But it was much closer to Mercatale, and so we didn't have to make such long journeys transporting the grapes and olives to the cellars and olive press. The village was close by for Franca to do her shopping and the boys had only a short walk to go to school. So we stayed there for another ten years. In 1966 my cousin Edoardo died. He had a brain tumour, poor fellow, and suffered a great deal. At that time my brother Azeglio was unable to work much because he had a bad knee, he could barely walk. So I was the only man left to work the farm: the boys were too small and Silvio, the *garzone*, could only carry out a limited number of jobs.

The situation became impossible. It is true that if I had been offered the chance to buy the farm I might have done so, whatever the *sacrificio*, as in a few years' time my sons would have been old enough to help me with the work. However, the new *padrone* didn't want to sell the property, but neither was he prepared to make those improvements to the house which would have made it more comfortable. Then Tono made a suggestion: 'Why don't you buy a flat in Pestello, down near Montevarchi? They're building some new blocks of flats there and they are going quite cheaply.' 'But Tono, I can't afford it!' I protested. 'The money I get from selling oil and wine is barely enough to keep my family!' 'I'll lend you what you need to make the first payment,' said Tono. He had more contacts than I did and had heard of the possibility of buying a house in instalments. 'Then you can find work in Florence as a builder's mate. All the building firms are looking for peasants because they are not afraid of hard work, they're not lazy like the townspeople. That way they'll take the instalments off your pay packet week by week, and you don't have to worry about it. As for the money I'll lend it to you. *'Per pagare e morire c'è sempre tempo.'* 'There's always time to pay and to die.'

A pay packet! By now I was forty-two years old and I had never received one. I began to reflect. I hated the idea of leaving the land, but there was no future for me on that farm and the thought of getting a pay packet every fortnight was most inviting. Franca and I discussed the matter that evening. She had no doubts about it: she was tired of doing a peasant woman's work from morning till evening. Also, she was beginning to get back pains and could no longer do the heavy work that was required of her.

So we made our decision. With Tono's help we bought a flat: it was on the third floor of a small block in a quiet street in Pestello, only half a mile from Montevarchi. I got a job with a building firm in Florence, and, as Tono had told me, within a few years I was able to finish paying for the flat, and could also pay him back the money he had lent me. I took the train to Florence five days a week. I had to get up very early, as I had to take a train at half past four in the morning in order to get to my workplace by seven: but I was used to getting up early. Being a builder's mate was hard work, as I had to serve two builders, going back and forth with a wheelbarrow to supply them with the necessary bricks and cement. But there again, I was used to hard work, I had done it all my life. At weekends I could rest. I could even enjoy the luxury of staying in bed an extra hour, something I hadn't been able to do once during the thirty years I had been a peasant. Even better, now, finally, I felt free!

Glossary

aia   threshing-floor; flat area near farmhouse where haystacks, strawricks and woodpiles are located

a pinzimonio   the eating of raw vegetables such as artichokes dipped in a mixture of olive oil, salt and pepper

aretino   cold east wind blowing from the direction of Arezzo

Balilla   car produced by Fiat in 1932; member of the Fascist youth organization

Befana   derives from *Epifania*, Epiphany. This ugly but benevolent witch is not peculiar to Italy, as Pietro suggests, but can be found among the traditions of France, Germany and England

Beltordo   Pietro's version of Bertoldo, the hero of the novel *Bertoldo e Bertoldino*, written by G.C. della Croce (1550–1609). Stories of this picaresque figure were very popular in the countryside

Berlingaccio   last day of Carnival, the last Thursday before Shrove Tuesday. Also the symbolic figure that represented it, a fat, jolly, red-faced fellow

bersagliere (pl. *bersaglieri*)   *bersaglieri* are soldiers belonging to a regiment founded in 1836 and are renowned for their courage. Their uniform includes a jaunty hat with a plume. The regiment band performs the *fanfara* at a brisk trot, not easy for those playing wind instruments

bigone (pl. *bigoni*)   container used in wine-making. It is waist-high and is made of wooden staves

bottega (pl. *botteghe*)   small shop selling basic foodstuffs. In small villages it also serves as a bar

burischio   sausage made of pig's blood

canonica   priest's house beside the church

capaccia   large sausage made mostly of parts taken from the pig's head

capoccio   head of a peasant family

carabiniere (pl. *carabinieri*)   policeman whose special duty is to maintain public order and enforce observance of the law. He wears a distinctive navy-blue uniform with a red stripe down the side of the trousers

casa colonica   sharecropper's house

casa padronale   landowner's mansion

centesimo   one-hundredth of a lira

cicogna   literally 'stork'; a small reconnaissance plane

Comune   municipality, in this case that of Montevarchi

companatico   from the Latin *cum pane*, something eaten with bread

conca   large, wide-rimmed, earthenware vase

contadino   farmer of low social status, either the owner of his land or a sharecropper

contrasti   contest, once common in the Tuscan countryside, in which two poets, usually illiterate, were given a theme and, taking opposing viewpoints, extemporized in *ottava rima*

correggiato   flailing tool, from *correggia*, fart

crocifisso   crucifix; shrine containing image of Christ on the cross

cucina economica   wood stove, still used in the countryside

Duce   leader, from the Latin *dux*, the title Mussolini assumed when he came to power in 1922

fattoria (pl. *fattorie*) derives from *fattore*, farm bailiff, and means the big estate which he administered

figli e figlie della Lupa literally, sons and daughters of the wolf. In Roman mythology a she-wolf nursed the twins Romulus and Remus. Later Romulus founded the City of Rome and the she-wolf became its symbol. The Fascists took a lot of their inspiration from classical Rome, hence the name of this organization for small children

finocchiona typical Tuscan salami, made of pork and fennel seeds

frantoiano workman responsible for the production of olive oil at the *frantoio*, olive press

gabbie circular reed mats used at the olive press

garzone unpaid labourer, usually a young boy from a poor peasant family

governo part of the wine-making process, peculiar to Tuscany, whereby grapes are added to the must to bring about a second fermentation

grandinina literally, small hailstones: a kind of pasta used in soups

grappa Brandy distilled from the fermented residue of grapes

graticcio (pl. *graticci*) tray made from wild clematis stems woven together within a chestnut wood frame: nothing placed on it would go bad because air circulated underneath it

guardie campestri field wardens

innocentini children from the *Innocenti* orphanage in Florence

loppio field maple, *acer campestre*, a small tree taken from the wild and pruned in the shape of a candelabra to support vines

madia piece of furniture found in all peasants' houses: it resembled a chest with legs, and bread was kneaded inside it

malinpeggio   literally, 'from bad to worse', a humorous name for a tool which at one end was a small axe and a hollowed-out pick at the other

Maremma   area in south-east Tuscany famous for its cornfields, cattle, dogs and horses

marrone (pl. *marroni*)   large chestnut with plenty of flavour, used for boiling or roasting. The smaller *castagna* chestnut is used principally for making chestnut flour

massaia   housewife in a peasant family

mezzadria   agricultural system dating from the Middle Ages whereby a landowner would provide the machinery, seed and so on and the sharecropper would supply the labour

mezzadro (pl. *mezzadri*)   from *mezzo*, half: sharecropper

Monte de' Pasqui di Siena: famous bank of Siena, founded in 1472. Over the centuries it played a leading role as patron of the arts

norcino   man from Norcia, in Umbria, where many pork-butchers came from

olio di sansa   inferior olive oil made at the end of the pressing process and now not usually used for human consumption

ottava rima   eight-lined stanza with the rhyme scheme 'aba-babcc'. It was the traditional verse-form for narrative poetry: Ariosto used in *Orlando Furioso*. In Pietro's day local poets used this stanza for their improvisations

padrone (pl. *padroni*)   master or landowner

paletti   small stakes

Palio   famous horse race that takes place twice a year in Piazza del Campo, the main square of Siena. The city is divided into 17 *quartieri*, or neighbourhoods, and each one has a symbol which distinguishes its banners: a giraffe, a tortoise, a wave, a tower and so on. The *quartieri* draw lots for the ten places in

the race. The prize is a *palio*, a banner specially made for the
occasion

panzanella summer dish made of stale bread that has been
soaked in water, oil, vinegar, tomatoes, onions and basil

pecorino Tuscany's most typical cheese, made from sheep's milk

picce dried figs with aniseed inside

Piccole Italiane young Italian girls belonging to a Fascist youth
organization

pieve mother church with minor churches under its jurisdiction
and the only one with a baptismal font

pigionali rentpayers, considered unfortunate because they had
no land

podere (pl. *poderi*) sharecropper's farmhouse with on average
thirty to forty acres of land round it

Podestà medieval term used by the Fascists to denote the mayor

porcino *boletus edulis*, the most prized of wild mushrooms

prete literally, 'priest'; a bedwarmer using embers from the fire

ricciaia pit dug in the woods to store the chestnuts

riccio prickly husk of a chestnut

sacrificio hard work carried out for a worthy cause, such as
educating one's children

sfollato voluntary evacuee

squadristi members of a Fascist action squad, known for their
brutality

staio (pl. *staia*) wooden vessel for measuring cereals and pulses.
Its size varied from region to region

tagliatelle e maccheroni pasta made with flour, eggs and water.
Tagliatelle are long, thin strips, *maccheroni* are broader and
shorter

tramontana strong and bitterly cold wind blowing from the
north-east, often bringing snow

vasche large shallow earthenware bowls used when making olive oil

veglia literally, 'the state of being awake'. It came to mean the evenings peasants spent sitting round the fire and entertaining themselves. The custom has disappeared since the arrival of television

vinaccia dregs of pressed grapes

vinsanto sweet white wine made of dried grapes, typical of Tuscany and Umbria. It is used during the celebration of Mass

zappa tool that is a cross between a hoe and a spade, suitable for the heavy terrain of the area. It has become the symbol of backbreaking labour